Elizabeth H. Cotter

Elizabeth H. Cotter

COLOR PHOTOGRAPHY

Eliot Elisofon

COLOR

PHOTOGRAPHY

◼ *A Studio Book*

The Viking Press   New York

ACKNOWLEDGMENTS

I am indebted to Herbert Orth, chief of the *Life* Color Laboratory, for his assistance in checking certain of the technical data, and also for preparing the special charts for this volume.

I would also like to thank Bryan Holme of The Viking Press for giving special guidance and effort in the planning and production of this book and *Life* magazine for granting permission to use the color plates.

This book would not have been possible without the cooperation of the many persons I have worked with in almost every part of the globe. I am especially appreciative of the instruction, help, and inspiration I have received from my colleagues, past and present, and I would like to dedicate this book to all of them, especially to those who have passed on.

CONTENTS

FOREWORD

Eliot Elisofon started photography with a box Brownie belonging to his sister, when he was in high school. "Even then," he says, "I had an interest in painting, and when I discovered that the camera was a new way to draw without training, I made more and more photographs which I thought resembled paintings. My so-called photographs and I went through successive stages of cameras until, upon graduation from college, I decided to become a professional photographer. I doubt if anyone was less trained for this career than I."

His achievements since then would scarcely bear out that statement, unless we argue that good artists are born, not trained. This is probably true.

His first real break came from the magazine *Mademoiselle*, which gave him and his partner, Martin Bauman, the shopping column to illustrate. This led to some fashion work, in 1936 to an assignment to cover a big society ball, and in 1937 to his first exhibition—composed mostly of off-beat pictures of New York—held at the New School for Social Research. I chose a photograph from this show to run on a spread in *U.S. Camera*'s annual.

Alexie Brodovitch, art director of *Harper's Bazaar*, was impressed by Eliot's work and showed it to Carmel Snow, the editor, who found it too radical to publish in that magazine, so he steered Eliot on to *Life* Magazine. There followed many assignments, including regular ones commissioned by Wilson Hicks, the picture editor of *Life*. In 1938 Elisofon decided to devote himself exclusively to magazine photography. In 1942 he joined the *Life* staff to become a war photographer and has remained with the magazine ever since.

Eliot Elisofon has the distinction of being one of the few photographers *Life* credits in print for his picture stories, and readers of this book may remember such notable ones as "Literary South Seas," "Actors and Actresses in their Dream Roles," "European Restaurants," "The Oregon Coast," "Spring in Japan," "Jazz Portfolio," "Nigeria," and, among many others, several of the "America's Arts and Skills" series. And there was also that choice feature on *Moulin Rouge*, the film Eliot worked on as color consultant.

No other photographer has pioneered more in the field of color control, and he has filled this book with information on creative color photography that just about everybody, I would say, is going to have to read—and with enthusiasm, for here a whole new world of ideas and a great many new techniques are revealed.

Eliot Elisofon is one of America's finest and most versatile photographers. I can't think of a photographer more dedicated or more excited by his profession. This is a photographer—and the lack of adjectives in my notes is a tribute to one of the men who has made photo-journalism, and photography, the great and emphatic pursuit it is. Perhaps I should say he is a great photographer. More important, he is a human being who has found a lens the best delineator of all that's important to living. The pictures will tell you more than any words. The name is Eliot Elisofon —it rings with candor, humor, honesty, and humanity.

Tom Maloney
Editor of *U.S. Camera*

INTRODUCTION

For more than a hundred years people have been taking black-and-white photographs, and have come to accept as a matter of course the translation of natural colors into tones from black to white. But today photography has developed to the point where anyone can just as easily take photographs in color. We push the button and the laboratory does the rest. Both mediums, color and black-and-white, are at our disposal and it is up to us to choose which of the two suits our particular purpose the better. The person who is exclusively addicted to either one loses a means of expression in the art of photography. Both have their specific problems, and both their proper place.

Photography is not only one of the most useful forms of expression; it is one of the most beautiful. Furthermore, some cameras are so simple to operate that even children can make pictures, often with excellent results.

After twenty-five years devoted to photography, I still find it extraordinary that by pushing a button a machine will record whatever profound or trivial observation my consciousness has directed. Instead of laboriously making a free-hand drawing, which most of us are as incapable of doing as playing the violin, or writing an inadequate description of what we see and how we react to it, the camera in a fraction of a second can capture forever on film the exact images we wish.

Of course, not everyone, creatively speaking, has something to say, or even wishes to say it. Most people are happy enough to make color photographs simply as a record. They give little or no thought to technique or esthetics; they make snapshots of trips, friends, pets, without ever thinking that such photographs, handled creatively, might result in material worthy of an exhibition or of reproduction in a magazine.

9

It would be a mistake to encourage everyone who owns a camera to believe he can become an artist overnight, but I feel the more that is known about the ins and outs of photography, the greater the satisfaction of every individual who practices it. I have therefore attempted in this book to spell out in simple language, for amateur and professional alike, what I myself have learned about color photography, and the reasons why I recommend this or that procedure.

The illustrations on the following pages range from the simplest outdoor snapshot to photographs involving tons of equipment; one, for example, took no less than three days, five men, two radio police cars, and ten truck drivers to make. There are others that took days of thought and five minutes to execute.

Since the invention of color photography, most of the discussion about it has been technical, and it is rare to find anyone writing about it in terms of esthetics; yet this, in the end, is the determining factor between distinguished and run-of-the-mill results. We have been flooded with calendars and postcards in which color has not portrayed nature faithfully, much less interpreted it. The plethora of uniform, clean, well-exposed pictures with bright blue skies has reached a monotony of millions, and the few interesting deviations have been due mostly to the accidents of nature. "Get the sun over your left shoulder, set the exposure for 1/50th at F5.6, push the button, and the lab does the rest." From this advice has come a stream of snapshots that are not unpleasant to look at but cannot be termed art. I believe that anyone who has done something well wants either to do better next time or to try something new. There is no end to the fascinating effects that can be achieved in color photography, and a book that goes a little deeper into these possibilities seems to me long overdue. Hence this present attempt.

First, there is the question of the purpose of a given photograph. If it is meant to be a scientific record, the photographer must do all he can to produce a photographic image as close to what he sees as he possibly can with the films and equipment now available on the market. A photographer making a document of the Sistine Chapel does not have the privilege of changing the colors or perspective to suit his own ideas. But in photo-journalism a primary consideration has always been: Where does originality begin and reporting end? This does not mean that mechanical perfection is necessarily honest. It is well established that a color photograph can be different from the human eye's impression of the same scene. The question of which is more real—actuality or a pointing up of actuality to make the subject more understandable to the spectator—is a problem which must be resolved by the doer himself.

The color photographer, who of necessity works with a mechanical object, the camera, is very often taken over by the instrument and film. Does he ever wish that a sky were less bright blue, that a softer tone would be better with the principal subject in the photograph? Does he yearn for the addition of a slight warm tone over the entire composition in order to pull the various colors together and mute them into a harmonious whole, as the thin umber and sienna glazes do in Renaissance painting? I believe in color selection and color control. I believe that the photographer has the privilege and the right to interpret his subject. He should not be a mechanic producing near-facsimiles of nature in random fashion, without thought or taste. The discriminating photographer, by his choice of subject, of time of day, of light and other effects, can exercise important control on the production of the image. My belief is that the photographer can do anything he wishes, provided the result is in keeping with the thought or idea he wants to express. The photograph must be an image organic to the nature of the material. This is a basic concept common to all art.

The photographer, like any other artist, needs proper tools for his work. Also, he must be able to employ them precisely, in order to execute his ideas. Craftsmanship is essential. When correctly manipulated, the tools of photography are capable of making pictorial images that are richer in detail, texture and tonal range, and more striking in perspective than most hand-made pictures are. This is part of the joy of working in this medium. And, in addition to the physical beauty that photography is capable of achieving, there is also the ability of the camera to capture, as fast as the blink of an eye, precious and important events, vignettes of daily life, and the wonder of the world around us.

In any analysis of color photography we come face to face with the most basic question: what is the significance of color itself? Does one color mean one thing and another something else? Are we affected by color? Does it make any difference? The answers to these questions have occupied experts for a long time. One of the most useful sources of information on this subject is a book, *Film Sense*, (New York: Harcourt, Brace, 1942) written by the Soviet film director Sergei Eisenstein, who, along with the American D. W. Griffith did more to develop the art of the cinema than anyone else.

Writers have contributed many observations on the significance of color, but it is probably from painters that we can learn the most, for they rely on color as much as they do on form to produce a desired effect. Photographers can make use of color as painters do, and indeed painting and photography (in the truly artistic use of it) are so closely related that their influences often overlap.

Yellow is one of the most interesting colors, regarding both use and theory. Havelock Ellis notes that in the early Christian period yellow was the color of jealousy, envy, and treachery. He mentions that in sixteenth-century France the doors of traitors were daubed with yellow. In Spain, confessed heretics carried yellow crosses and candles. French slang assigns the color yellow to deceived husbands. Americans refer to cowards as yellow. Hitler's Germany chose yellow for the Star of David which Jews were forced to wear. In the field of painting Van Gogh, who fortunately wrote many letters about his work, describes the use of yellow in one of his paintings, "The Night Café," in terms of its psychological significance. He wrote that "to express the powers of darkness and evil" he employed the color of pale sulphur to suggest "an atmosphere like a devil's furnace." Van Gogh carefully distinguished the shade of yellow—pale sulphur. He did this because sometimes it is not so much the question of a color as of which shade or hue of a color. Golden yellow is far different from sulphur yellow. Warm yellows suggest sunshine, ripening wheat, beautiful blond hair, even the color of highly prized gold. Walt Whitman constantly uses the word golden as a pleasant image. In another work, however, he understands how one color is affected by another nearby, when he says, "and the yellow-blue countenance..." He is writing about an unpleasant scene and describing a wound. Whitman could not have placed the two color words any closer; he hyphenates them in his desire to set up an unpleasant color harmony.

But painters best understand color juxtaposition. Orozco, the great Mexican muralist, in a large painting hanging in the Palace of Fine Arts in Mexico City, uses a bilious green edge-line on the pink torsos of naked prostitutes lying in front of a contemporary scene. The painting is his protest against capitalist society, and Orozco has tried to make the naked women more naked and more ugly by the use of clashing colors. Van Gogh in "The Night Café" uses a variety of greens. He describes them as "soft greens and malachite contrasting with yellow green and hard blue green" to further the impression that the café is an evil place. A window in the cathredral at Chartres depicts Satan with a green skin and green eyes. In the film *Moulin Rouge*, for which I helped devise the color effects, green was the color for unpleasantness and evil. Different shades of blue-green and green were used for varying situations, the blue-green for the dark street scenes in which Lautrec is limping around in the company of a streetwalker. The color changed to partly blue-green

and pure green in the studio sequence when he attempted suicide. These greens were made more acid in feeling by the inclusion of a gaudy pink lamp which he lighted upon entering the studio; the pink made the green appear much greener. In the scene where Lautrec fell down the stairs and in the dingy bar scene where he was drinking himself to death, pure green carried the unpleasant color to its utmost in these final sequences of the film. But does anyone know a more beautiful moment than the first green leaves of spring? It is always a question of association when an artist uses color.

The Japanese, in their great Kabuki theater, use blue, not green, to create a "sinister" impression. We all talk of "blue Mondays," or of feeling blue. I don't know if a person suffocating actually turns blue, but we all think so. The American Indian associates blue with the sky, with eternity, and, therefore, with death. In contrast, blue also has pleasant connotations: true blue, blue blood, for example. The highly desired baby boy is usually covered with blue clothing.

Red we think of as the color of vigor and violence. It actually suggests blood. During the last days of the French Revolution the remaining aristocrats carried red handkerchiefs as a reminder of the guillotine's blood-letting. We give the color red to revolutionaries and use the word red to describe a Communist. Although a bull will react to any moving cloth, the use of red has been traditional in bull-fighting. We speak of an angry man's seeing red and a bankrupt one's going into the red.

Purple has always been associated with gaudy prose and with royalty, and is also related to death. Richard Brooks, a Hollywood director with a great feeling for color, utilized purple in the magnificent death scene in his *Brothers Karamazov*. Sibyl Moholy-Nagy, in her biography of her late husband, writes about his paintings which he made just before he died: "...and there was a predominance of purple, graded from a delicate rose color to a dense violet. Some psychiatrists claim that an increased use of purple in the work of an artist indicates a subconscious death anticipation. Moholy knew nothing of this theory, but purple and a contrapuntal variation of greens are predominant among the rich production of August 1946" (*Moholy-Nagy;* New York: Harper, 1950, p.231). Note here, too, the word "contrapuntal," indicating the use of contrasting and conflicting colors.

Even a cursory glance through the illustrations of this book will, I think, reveal to the reader my predeliction for harmonious colors. I do not like to set one color against another, unless it is for a special purpose, such as in the picture of Hermione Gingold in the role of a witch (page 41). Harmony in color is very often the lack of strong contrast, especially with the primaries. It is usually achieved by working in different shades that blend with one another as do tan, russet, orange, and dark brown, or pink, red, and white. Color photographs I like best are often almost monochromatic, and at first glance might seem hardly worth four color plates for reproduction. But were they to be reproduced in black and white, most of the subtleties would be gone.

What conclusions do we come to from all this? It is clear that color can be used for more purposes than mere decoration. It can be selected equally for dramatic effects and subtle ones, to convey a feeling of conflict or tranquility, evil or well-being, happiness or sadness, intimacy or remoteness, warmth or coolness, masculinity or femininity, and so on. It is close to music in its effect upon the sensibilities of the audience. In the hands of the creative photographer controlled color can add a fine dimension to a flexible medium.

◨ 1

COLOR VERSUS
BLACK AND WHITE

The important question, posed earlier, is whether to make photographs in color or black-and-white. Both films are universally available, and the higher cost of color is seldom the determining factor. Photographers, then, must choose between the two for specific reasons. There are few small cameras which permit the interchangeability of different film carriers; were this not so, both types of film could be used at will in one camera. However, most large cameras take either individual film holders or different film backs, and many photographers find them a happy answer to the problem. Some advanced amateurs and most professionals own at least two 35mm camera boxes with a group of interchangeable lenses, and load each box with a different kind of film.

We are not primarily concerned with the making of motion pictures, but this question—when to film in color and when in black-and-white—has been very im-portant in the minds of film directors such as Elia Kazan, George Stevens, and Daniel Mann. These men have made most of their successful films in black-and-white despite the fact that the large-screen color movie is usually a more effective box-office attraction. The reason for their decision can be seen in such films as *On the Waterfront*, *A Place in the Sun*, and *The Rose Tattoo*, all of which were based on powerful personal drama and social realism. They say that the mere presence of color is often so romantic that the strong impact of a tense or violent scene is lost through prettiness. I appreciate their point of view. Most movie color is simply decoration. Black-and-white photography has a built-in power because of the simplicity of its image. The rich tones of black, white, and all the grays in between can be easily controlled through composition and lighting to produce psychological effects without the complications of color. It has also been suggested that for black-and-white films the audience supplies its own color.

I believe that color can be planned and controlled so that it represents more than mere decoration or prettiness. It can be used to heighten tension, create ugliness, stress any mood the photographer desires. Just as motion-picture producers use music for various effects besides the romantic in their films, so can the photographer use color in a creative way.

Painters, who must of course concern themselves primarily with color, have not ignored the impact of black-and-white either. Picasso's powerful mural, "Guernica," an indictment of the Spanish Civil War, features tones of black, white, and gray. Goya, in commenting on the horrors of the Napoleonic period in Spain, chose black-and-white etchings to produce his dramatic *Disasters of War*. These and other artists recognized the strength of black itself in the pictorial image. Robert Capa also recognized it in his great photograph, "Mourning Women," made in Naples during World War II (page 147).

The photographer, therefore, must be aware of these differences and of the content of his subject material. If he feels that absence of color makes for a more powerful result, he may either work in black-and-white or mute his color scheme to an almost monochromatic effect. No one will contend that superior black-and-white photographs do not have great beauty. The magnificent prints produced by such masters as Edward Weston, Ansel Adams, and Eugene W. Smith might have had less impact in color.

The most obvious occasion to employ color film is when a subject would be meaningless or dull without it. "New Guinea Portrait" (page 18) depends almost entirely on the bizarre color of the native's facial decoration. The wild design of red, yellow, and black painted on his face relates in an interesting way with flowers of similar hue added to his headdress. In black-and-white this photograph would be far less effective. "Masked Ibo Dancers, Nigeria" (page 19) also demonstrates the necessity of color. Here the masks and costumes made of bright-colored cloth would be lost in black-and-white In addition, the color of the native costumes makes a strong contrast to the drab, incongruous World War I gas mask which has somehow found a place in the ceremony.

Interest need not depend solely on bright color. "Girl Bathing, Tahiti" (page 17) is an example of the simple color of nature, and the beautiful shades of her skin give the viewer a feeling of romance, which would be lacking in a black-and-white print. "Maine Lobsters," photographed at Vinalhaven (pages 22-23) is another case in point. Food has never looked appetizing in black-and-white, and here the use of color has been extended to stress the quiet atmosphere of a typical Maine harbor as well. The predominantly blue background sets off the color of the food and is echoed in the blue-patterned china. The view extending into the distance was deliberately kept sharp because every detail—the water, boats, lobster pots, floats, and fishermen all relate closely to the central theme.

Subtle color can sometimes capture more meaning than the most powerful hues. Two illustrations of this point are to be found in "Sacred Pond, Nara, Japan," (page 20) and "Father and Child, Nigeria" (page 21). In the photograph of the pond it was essential to capture the spirit of spring, and two important visual elements are present: the delicate, soft green of the first leaves of the weeping willow and the drops of rain falling into the pond. In the other photograph the portrait of the father and daughter is almost entirely monochromatic; only one obvious bit of color exists—the bright chemical green of the child's necklace, which stands out against the white and brown. This bit of color can be said to demonstrate the love of the father for his child, his desire to decorate and adorn her. A further comment on these two photographs is their relationship in color. Although the subjects were photographed at opposite sides of the globe, arranged next to each other in this layout they produce a harmonious double-page spread.

Four plates in color are contrasted with black-and-white by deliberate juxtaposition in this chapter. In the first, "Cherry Blossoms, Japan," (page 24) the pink is so soft that it is almost nonexistent. The color conveys the fragility and beauty of the blossoms. Appearing opposite this plate, and in great contrast, is the vigorous black-and-white "Head of Bakongo Fetish, Africa." "Coast of Chile" (page 28) also depends upon strong blacks and whites to convey the brooding quality of the coastline. This photograph, taken at sunset, used the low light to achieve solidity and form in the many rocks. A color photograph I made of the same scene a few moments earlier showed pink in the sky, which seemed to me out of character with the brutal coastline. "White Horse, Tahiti" (page 29) uses one color, green, to dramatize the whiteness of the horse and to illustrate the Nordhoff and Hall description of Tahiti (in *Mutiny on the Bounty*) as "a landscape... of some fantastic dream." It is the simplicity of color in this photograph which in my opinion produces its beauty.

A pair of portraits, both of artists, demonstrates how subject material dictated the choice of black-and-white in the one instance and color in the other. The portrait of the late Sir Jacob Epstein (page 30) was made in his London studio where old lumber and clay and plaster contributed no significant color. In contrast, the portrait of Morris Graves (page 31) depends almost entirely for its character on the muted greens of mosses and ferns which this artist employs in his own work. His choice of costume, faded denims, made blue-green by the excessive blue in the shady light, contributes to the overall color and general atmosphere appropriate to his character and particular style of painting.

Two other contrasting photographs were taken in Egypt. The one reproduced in color is of the Temple at Abu Simbel of Rameses II on the Nile (page 32). The poverty of color, with a shade of ocher for the figures cut into the cliff and the small piece of blue sky, gives the viewer a truer image of this great monument. It is also interesting to see the actual color of the stone. In the black-and-white photograph of the tomb of the son of Rameses II in Thebes (page 33), the natural colors were of much less interest. The sarcophagus was, in fact, almost colorless, and the walls were dark, dingy, and without the usual tomb decoration. Since very little light was used, part of the tomb was left in darkness. The placing of the front light gave shape and detail to the carved sarcophagus. The arrangement of blacks, whites, and grays—called chiaroscuro in the language of both photo-graphers and painters—produced an interesting effect. The background light was manipulated to keep the columns dark, so that a better visualization of a tomb was created.

The photograph of Margot Fonteyn (pages 26-27) and the Sadler's Wells Ballet was made from the prompter's box at the Metropolitan Opera House in New York. It was the first time such a thing had been permitted. Miss Fonteyn could hear the camera click, and she became so preoccupied with my timing in relationship to hers that she finally sent the assistant manager to ask me to desist, as it was interfering with her performance. This black-and-white picture has been included as an example of a candid photograph which was made quite easily with available light and in which the traditional white tutus of the dancers would have contributed little if anything in color.

The final photograph in this chapter, "Coast of Oregon," (pages 34-35) was taken at twilight. The last few strands of pink fade into the horizon under the impact of the deep blues which twilight produces on color film. It is this saturation of blue, plus the softness of the water's edge against the silhouetted black rocks, that gives the picture its atmosphere of mystery. Except for the blue, this photograph would have been equally successful as a black-and-white shot.

NOTES ON PLATES (pages 17-35)

17 GIRL BATHING, TAHITI.
Contax 11, 50mm Sonnar F1.5, 1/50 at f5.6, Skylight filter, Kodachrome.

18 NEW GUINEA PORTRAIT (NEAR MAPRIK).
Canon V, 85mm Canon F1.9, 1/125 at f5.6, Skylight filter, Kodachrome.

19 MASKED IBO DANCERS, NIGERIA.
Canon VI, 50mm Canon F1.8, 1/50 at f4, Skylight filter, Anscochrome.

20 SACRED POND, NARA, JAPAN.
Canon V, 35mm, Canon F1.9, 1/5 at f4, Skylight and CC-05 Y filters, Kodachrome.

21 FATHER AND CHILD, NIGERIA.
Canonflex, 50mm, Canon F1.8, 1/10 at f2, Kodachrome.

22-23 MAINE LOBSTERS.
5 × 7 Pico, 18cm Schneider Symmar F5.6, 1/10 at F32, Daylight Ektachrome. Two diffused # 50 B flashbulbs.

24 CHERRY BLOSSOMS, JAPAN.
Praktina, 58mm, Biotar F2, 1/50 at f4, Skylight filter, Kodachrome.

25 HEAD OF BAKONGO FETISH, AFRICA.
Linhof 4 × 5, 240mm Schneider Symmar, 10 seconds at F22, Super-xx pack. Lit with two RFI2 lamps. Tripod kicked during exposure. See diagram page 150.

26-27 MARGOT FONTEYN AND THE SADLER'S WELLS BALLET.
Contax II, 35mm, Biogon F2.8, 1/50 at f2.8, Super-xx film.

28 COAST OF CHILE.
Linhof 4 × 5, 135mm Ektar, f4.7, no record of exposure, Super-xx pack.

29 WHITE HORSE, TAHITI.
Contax II, 35mm Biogon F2.8, 1/50 at f8, Skylight filter, Kodachrome.

30 SIR JACOB EPSTEIN IN HIS LONDON STUDIO.
Linhof 4 × 5, 90mm Schneider Angulon F6.8, 1 second at F16, Super-xx pack. Daylight from studio windows plus two RFL2 lamps.

31 MORRIS GRAVES, IN NORTHWEST WOODS.
5 × 7 Deardorff, 180mm Schneider Symmar, 1/2 second at F16, Harrison B 1/8 filter, Ektachrome.

32 ABU SIMBEL, EGYPT.
Linhof 4 × 5, 127 Ektar F4.7, no record of exposure, Kodachrome.

33 MERENPTAH'S SARCOPHAGUS, THEBES, EGYPT.
4 × 5 Linhof, 90mm Schneider Angulon F6.8, 1/25 at f22, Super-xx pack. Two G.E. # 22 flash bulbs, one to right of figure, other behind column.

34-35 COAST OF OREGON.
5 × 7 Deardorff, 150mm Tessar F4.5, 10 seconds at f8, Ektachrome. Taken at twilight, no filters.

Opposite: RUINED PALACE OF
SANS SOUCI, HAITI.
*Speed Graphic $3\frac{1}{4} \times 4\frac{1}{4}$, 135mm Tessar
F4.5, no record of exposure, Kodachrome.*

◘ 2

COLOR CONTROL

The most obvious aspect of color control is also its single most important factor—the choice of subject. If you choose to photograph a girl in a bright red sweater, wearing an orange skirt, topped with a Kelly green hat, and pose her in front of a striped yellow and blue background, in full sunlight, then there really isn't much you—or anyone—can do to make this a harmonious color photograph, let alone an interesting or subtle one. You begin with what you photograph.

There are other choices to be made, not only in subject matter but in character, mood, and condition of light. For instance, the color value of daylight keeps changing, and a subject photographed at sunset will be warm in tone (page 60) while half an hour later, when the sun is completely down, the all-over effect will be blue. Natural outdoor lighting conditions provide an almost endless variety of effects.

Weather, too, is an important factor. The same scene will obviously photograph quite differently in sunshine and in rain. In addition, special color effects can be obtained outdoors as well as indoors by the use of various filters on cameras, or colored gelatins on lights, which will afford the photographer positive color control. These problems—I would rather call them opportunities—are treated in detail in the two chapters that follow. Meanwhile I should like to consider briefly here the whys and wherefores of color control and its history.

I had my earliest color assignments for *Life* in the late 1930s. One of my first subjects was the Appalachian Trail, and I made quite a few pictures of it without bright sunshine. These turned out surprisingly well. In 1941 I went to Hollywood and discovered that Harrison and Harrison had made some filters to control changes of color temperature (see page 153) in lighting. I purchased the

37

C series, which were coral in color and were meant to warm up the lighting. The B series (blue) were intended to do the opposite. I tried the filters several times indoors without much success. It was not until 1946 when I photographed the Palace of Sans Souci in Haiti (page 36) on a cloudy day, using the Harrison C½ filter, that I discovered the interesting effects this filter produced. The filters had been manufactured for indoor lighting, but this chance experiment of using one outdoors opened up a whole new phase of experiments. I first looked at the scene through the filter and then tried it on the camera. The result on the color film was slightly different, the filter color registering more in the darker parts of the subject than in the highlights, but the general effect was the same.

In 1946 I suggested to *Life* a feature on the Atlantic coastline from Maine to Florida. It was impossible to wait indefinitely for good weather, and fortunately some of the places I visited lent themselves well to fog and rain pictures. An example is shown on page 42 ("Race Point, Cape Cod"). The cape was extremely foggy that day, and after reviewing the situation I decided that without corrective filters the beach photograph would turn out too blue. I viewed the scene through a Harrison C½ filter and decided to use it. The interesting result, reproduced in *Life*, was my first published color-controlled photograph.

The following year, while on location in Europe, I again resorted to the use of filters. Instead of using a coral filter for "Sailboats in the Bay of Biscay" (page 43), I decided on a light yellow one, the Wratten K1. This was an arbitrary step, and I did it more from a desire for interpretation than as an attempt to remove excessive blue from the light. However, I was guided in the choice by my feeling that the coast of Spain and the old ships were out of the romantic past, and I wanted the photograph to be in the spirit of an old-master painting.

The subject of color control came up one evening in my home when Wilson Hicks, then the picture editor of *Life*, Miguel Covarrubias, the artist and archaeologist, and René d'Harnoncourt, director of the Museum of Modern Art, were looking at my European pictures. Hicks, who was one of the most important men in the early development of photo-journalism, said that I was overstepping my privileges as a magazine photographer by exercising this type of control. On the other hand, both Covarrubias and d'Harnoncourt came vehemently to my defense. D'Harnoncourt made the point that all art was subjective and that even the placing of a painting in one or another position on a museum wall created a quite different effect because of the relationship of the architecture and the color of the neighboring paintings.

To this day the question of color control and its honesty is a subject that occupies many people. I have never hesitated to interpret a scene, provided the interpretation was in character with the subject itself and with the mood I wished to create. If a treatment of the subject makes it understandable to an audience and does not distort its own intrinsic values, I consider that effect honest. And then there is another point to consider. The color film we begin with is far from perfect and incapable of producing an exact replica of nature; therefore it is extremely difficult to draw a straight line between reality and interpretation. Furthermore, by the time a color print or color reproduction has been made from a color transparency, the colors are already different from those on the transparency—sometimes only slightly different, but often very much so; thus interpretation comes into play here, too.

No one has seriously quarreled with the photographer who controls black-and-white, which in itself is, of course, an interpretation of color. Nor does anyone argue over which filter is used to darken a sky, or the off-eye level angle at which a photograph may be taken, or about the use of a wide-angle or telephoto lens. The use of all these devices is part of the photographer's art in getting the most out of particular scenes. One might go further and ask, Are posed photographs fakes even if they look more candid than snapshots? Are indoor available-light photographs the only honest portrayal of a scene, even if we can't see what it is? It would seem to me that individual judgment, not inflexible rules, must determine the extent of the photographer's control. For years we have had a movement where the aim of the photographer was to make photographs that looked like anything except a photograph. One of the most disheartening things in photography can be its coldly mechanical perfection. It takes a fine artist to give photography the kind of life, warmth, and individuality that is acclaimed in other mediums of expression.

On the two films on which I worked as color consultant—*Moulin Rouge* and *Bell, Book, and Candle*, color control seemed suitable, in order to heighten the dramatic quality of the stories. Color was used not for its own sake but to underline and reinforce the ideas of the writer and to assist the director in conveying those ideas to the audience. The techniques used in filming *Moulin Rouge* may be of interest to readers who make home movies.

To get the story and mood firmly in my mind, I read the *Moulin Rouge* film scenario several times; then I read various biographies of and articles about Lautrec. I went to Albi, the artist's birthplace, and studied the house where he was born and the surrounding countryside.

I looked at his paintings in the local museum. I also studied anew his paintings in Paris and reproductions of many other examples of his work. I had decided that in spite of Lautrec's genius as a painter, it would be an error to attempt too slavish a copy of his pictorial style and color. It was necessary to create the spirit of Lautrec, with any visual means available. In writing the color scenario I assigned specific shades to each of the principal actors. Toulouse-Lautrec, for instance, was always to be photographed with light blue-green "fill" light (which increases light in a shadow area), just enough to stain the shadow side of his face and figure; this gave him a definite color symbol. The fashion model he fell in love with was assigned soft pink.

I spent more than two weeks making a series of experimental color photographs of various subjects to be featured in the film, including a horse event at Fontaine-bleau, a group of can-can dancers in a Paris café, an artist's studio, and a street scene at dawn. Each scene or object was photographed through filters and with lighting that employed a variety of colored gelatins over the lamps. Four tests made before the filming of *Moulin Rouge* are reproduced on pages 46-47. "Paris Street Scene" is shown in two variations—yellow and blue. The yellow test was made by loading the film with the emulsion down instead of up in the holder. The same effect could also have been achieved with a yellow filter such as the K 2. The blue test was made with incandescent color film during daylight. The same effect could have been made on daylight color film with a Harrison B½ filter. "Girl on Bridge" is also seen two ways: without any filter (page 46) and with a light yellow filter, the K 1 (page 47).

All the test photographs for *Moulin Rouge* were shown to John Huston, the director, to Marcel Vertès, the gifted painter who was art director of the film, and to Ossie Morris, the cameraman. A color plan for the entire movie was accepted and the sets, costumes, camera filters, and gelatins were coordinated before the final shooting began. Two weeks were spent with a Techni-color camera trying out all the filters and gelatins outdoors and indoors on pieces of fabric, on patches of wall paint, on actors' make-up, to be certain that everything worked according to plan. The most important element, *constancy*, was agreed upon. In color-controlled filming it is important not to confuse the audience by changing the colors with which certain moods and characters become associated.

One of the developments in *Moulin Rouge* was the differentiation between warm and cool color. All the happy boyhood scenes were coral-filtered to make these sequences warm and intimate; later on in the film the unhappy dark street scenes were filtered in cool colors to create an opposite impression.

The portrait of Hermione Gingold (page 41), dressed as the chief witch in *Bell, Book, and Candle*, was made on the Columbia set after the cameraman had completed a film sequence. By turning off the huge battery of lights which are necessary for most actions, I was able to make this portrait with just one spot and one flood. The spot, which was off to the side, had a light pink gelatin, and the diffused flood near the camera had a light blue-green. The choice of color for Miss Gingold, both in costume and make-up, had been worked out with Jean Louis, who designed the costumes. The orange-red hair was chosen because we wanted her to look appropriately weird. To heighten the ghastly effect we selected a dress with purple splotches that would fight with the orange. A viridian green (barely seen in this photograph) was used on the background to contribute to the over-all spookiness.

The special problems and privileges of film-making are not shared by all photographers. No better craftsmen exist than those in Hollywood, but it often takes more than craftsmanship to know which control is necessary or useful, and how to use it. To readers who saw the film *South Pacific*, in which a person singing outdoors changes from red to purple to several other shades for no reason whatsoever, it should be clear how dangerous color control may be. Had the effects been really beautiful, few people would have quarreled. It is better to forget about color control than to misuse it.

The choice of film emulsion is also an important factor in color control. The type of film dictates different grain size, contrast, and actual color rendition. The new High Speed Ektachrome with which the photographs on pages 44 and 45 were made is characterized by coarse grain but softer contrast, as well as a film speed fast enough to work with dim available lighting. The grain in this instance is not undesirable, and the high speed is essential for this effect. No filters were used for these two pictures.

In still photography, which is what the majority of readers are likely to concern themselves with most, my advice at the beginning is to try out color filters when the subject suggests an improved or interesting result through their use, but to take straight shots as well, so that the possibility of disappointment is avoided. Viewing a scene by eye through a filter makes it possible to gauge approximately what the camera will record when the same filter is placed over the lens. Actually, the color effect on film is slightly lighter than as the eye sees it through the filter, and the filter tone shows more strongly in the shadows. It should be remembered that the length of exposure has to be adjusted to correspond with the density of the filter.

NOTES ON PLATES (pages 41-47)

41   HERMIONE GINGOLD IN
Bell, Book, and Candle.

Canon VI, 85mm Canon F1.9, 1/50 at f4, Kodachrome A. Film studio lights, one with pink gelatin, other blue-green.

42   RACE POINT, CAPE COD.

Linhof 4 × 5, 150mm Tessar F4.5, 1/10 at f11, Harrison C ¼, Kodachrome.

43   SAILBOATS IN THE BAY OF BISCAY.

Linhof 4 × 5, 240mm Schneider Symmar, 1/25 at f8, Wratten K1 filter, Kodachrome.

44   FOLLIES, NICHIGEKI THEATRE, TOKYO.

Nikon F, 58mm F1.4, 1/30 at F1.4, High Speed Ektachrome (tungsten). Actual theatre lighting.

45   GEISHA HOSTESSES, URUBASHI NIGHT CLUB, TOKYO.

Nikon F, 58mm F1.4, 1/8 second at F1.4, High Speed Ektachrome (tungsten). Light from cigarette lighter plus one bounce flood with light blue gelatin on a white cardboard, held 4 feet from subject.

46   (a) PARIS STREET SCENE, YELLOW.

Deardorff 5 × 7, 15cm Tessar F4.5, 1/2 second at f11, Daylight, Ektachrome, loaded emulsion side down.

(b) PARIS STREET SCENE, BLUE.

Deardorff 5 × 7, 15cm Tessar F4.5, 1 second at f11, Ektachrome B (tungsten).

(c) GIRL ON BRIDGE, PARIS.

Rolleiflex, 75mm Tessar F3.5, 1/50 at f6.3, no filter, Ektachrome.

47   GIRL ON BRIDGE, PARIS.

Automatic Rolleiflex, 75mm Tessar F3.5, 1/50 at f5.6, Wratten K1 filter, Ektachrome.

a

b

c

48

◘ 3

TIME OF DAY
AND WEATHER

The time of day we choose to make a picture and the kind of light we use are most important. Sunlight pictures are totally different from those made in the shade, and each hour brings with it a significant change in the quality of color.

Color photography may start before the sun has come into view. If you can see the subject you can also photograph it—taking the usual precaution of checking the right exposure with your meter. Whereas you may be experienced in judging daytime exposures, early and late daylight are trickier.

Early daybreak and late twilight are saturated with blue; consequently photographs made at either of these times of day are correspondingly blue in tone. An example of this is to be seen in the photograph of the Lincoln Memorial (pages 54-55). This subject is so well known that one of my tasks was to find a way of inter-

preting it differently. The assignment *Life* gave me was to illustrate a feature on Harry S. Truman's memoirs. After several conferences it was decided to photograph Washington as the President saw it on his famous early-morning walks. As a result the pre-dawn and dawn scenes I photographed gave the Lincoln Memorial and other familiar sights in Washington quite a new look. The blue effect obtained by shooting before dawn was selected for Lincoln because blue is serene and, I felt, a more appropriate color for the subject than the yellows and oranges which come with the dawn itself. To soften the image, I used a Harrison #3 fog filter which also produced a misty effect and heightened the feeling of dawn.

An actual dawn shot is the panorama view "Teton Range" (pages 56-57). The bluish effect discussed above can be observed in the trees, but where the first rays of sun are touching them (at the extreme left of the picture) a warm yellow tinge may be seen. I achieved this photograph after climbing to the same lookout point for three days in a row before dawn, each time in the hope of getting a dawn shot with low-hanging clouds around the great mountains. At midday the Tetons are magnificent, but a photograph made then would look like the millions of others that have been made of this famous beauty spot. Dawn also gave an interesting hue to the mountains, a soft pink, which again produced an unusual image.

Mid-morning and mid-afternoon create very much the same color effects. Shadows are generally deep, and the light is closest in balance with the normal color range of daylight film. At best it is a neutral light. "Yap Girl Dancing" (page 53) is an example of the simple quality of mid-morning light. Another example, of another girl, "Girl Bathing, Tahiti" (page 17) was made at about the same time of day. In this case I used a Kodak Skylight filter to give a warmer skin effect.

During the morning and afternoon there is also the opportunity of working with backlighting. As a rule the best time to use backlighting is in the early morning or late afternoon, but not so close to sunrise or sunset that too warm a tone results. When shooting into the light instead of by the conventional method of photographing with the light source behind the camera, a lens hood or some other form of protection must be used so that the sun does not strike the lens and cause halation.

Generally speaking, the most uninteresting time of day, and also the most difficult for color photography, is high noon. The light comes directly or almost directly from above, depending on the season and place, and flat, dull landscapes are a common result. Portraits made outdoors at high noon suffer from deep black shadows in the hollows of the face, as well as squinty eyes. However, a corrective here can be the use of reflectors to light the shadow part of the face.

Many photographers do not make exposures during this midday period. I very seldom do, but there are exceptions to every rule. I photographed "Bits and Spurs" (pages 58-59) at high noon so that all the shadows cast by the many small objects fell directly below each piece, eliminating the possibility of too many long shadows that would detract from the objects themselves.

The warm lighting of sunset, as well as that of sunrise, can greatly enrich a subject. In Nigeria I had a chance to photograph a group of young Miango girls dancing (pages 60-61). The girls began dancing in late afternoon and went on past sunset. The difference in effect between the straight color shots I took at the beginning and those I took later in the yellow light of the sunset (reproduced here) was enormous. It took the warm light to bring out the supple loveliness of their bodies and to convey a glowing mood to the entire scene. The characteristic long shadows, incidentally, greatly help the composition.

In the same country I made another photograph at sunset, "Women Pounding Grain" (page 75), which also benefited from the warm light. In this instance, however, I used a light-yellow filter to further the effect.

Twilight, both photographically and spiritually, is to me the most interesting time of the day. During this brief period there is a quietness and serenity in most landscapes which transform even ordinary scenes into magical images. "Coast of Oregon" (pages 34-35) was made at twilight, and so was "Canoes and Torchlight" (pages 62-63). Twilight lasts but a few minutes, so the photographer must work fast. In these few minutes a photograph may be made in which almost all detail but the highlights is absent. Underexposure slightly earlier in the evening may sometimes create the same impression and, if you arrive soon enough at the location to be photographed, it is worth experiment.

In the torch scene two things had to show—the shape of the peak against the sky, and the differentiation between water and mountain, both of which form the pictorial backdrop for the torches. The photograph illustrates the scene Gauguin wrote about in *Noa Noa*—"The families of the fishermen were awaiting us on the sand on the edge of the illumined water. Some of the figures remained seated and motionless; others ran along the shore waving the torches, . . ." This passage gave me the necessary directions for the people who had volunteered to be photographed. The exposure had to be correct for sky and water, underexposing the detail of the silhouetted mountain. Torches were constructed, canoes rented, and a rehearsal was held all afternoon to re-enact Gauguin's scene. As it turned out, the four canoes came into the shore one behind the other, and the whole scene had to be rephotographed the following day because the twilight just didn't last long enough to get the canoes back into the proper position for a retake.

I believe that the Samoan beach picture was the first color photograph (page 64) made by moonlight ever to be published in a magazine. Although there is almost no color in "Palms and Moonlight," a subtle, soft tone pervades the atmosphere and comes through in the reproduction. Moonlight color pictures have to be taken as time exposures. In this instance I gave it ten seconds at f2, using Kodachrome film.

The time of day is not so important if the sun is not shining. The photograph of a shy Japanese bride (page 48) was made in the afternoon of a slightly overcast day. The same effect could be achieved on a sunny day by taking the subject in light shade, such as under a tall tree or on a veranda. Hollywood technicians often use large pieces of thin cheesecloth stretched on long poles, which, when held over the heads of the actors, cut down the sharpness of the sunlight. Pictures made in the shade or on slightly overcast days normally require the use of a Kodak Skylight filter to remove some of the excess blue light which is present. No increase in exposure is necessary with this filter. There will be times when you are content with an exaggeration of blue, but usually pictures taken under either of these conditions should be color-corrected. A Skylight filter was used for the photograph of Ueno Park in Tokyo (page 65) made during a light rain. In cases of heavy rain a double Skylight filter is more efficient in cutting down the bluish cast.

Some photographers keep a Skylight filter on the lens at all times regardless of weather. Although I am against this type of generalization it is better to have the filter on all the time than never to use it. In addition to the Kodak Skylight filter, it is possible to obtain stronger and slightly different effects with the Harrison series. The coral filters, known as the C Series, come in various strengths: $\frac{1}{8}$, $\frac{1}{4}$, $\frac{1}{2}$, 1, and 2. I rarely use more than the $\frac{1}{8}$ or $\frac{1}{4}$. These filters will remove the excessive blue during heavy clouds or rain and may also contribute a slight amount of umber to the over-all quality of the picture. I did not use the Harrison C$\frac{1}{8}$ for the Ueno Park scene because I did not want to create this effect on the pure black lanterns or to change the attractive color of the raincoat. The Skylight filter provided the correct effect. In the rain photograph of the Nara pond (page 20) the Skylight filter once more was used. This same filter was used with interesting results in photographing the calumet yearlings at Lexington, Kentucky (pages 76-77).

An example of permitting the excess blue in shade to create a pleasing effect was discussed earlier and demonstrated in the portrait of Morris Graves (page 31). Here the blue added richness to his clothes and to the foliage in front of him.

A relatively infrequent occurrence is a scene in which both sunlight and heavy clouds are present; I encountered this situation while photographing the Shelburne Museum in Vermont (pages 66-67). Since no filter was used, the red buildings in sunshine were properly exposed and the bluish cast of the storm clouds was effectively retained.

Snow is another special problem, and a common one. In strong sunshine the shadows especially have a tendency to go blue in photography. This effect may be quite pretty and desirable in some instances, but when it is not desirable the Skylight filter will usually give adequate control. Here, as in every other case, individual photographers develop their own preferences after experimenting fully both with and without filters under every kind of weather condition.

From all the foregoing we can come to some conclusions about time of day and weather. The primary reason for our choice depends upon the subject. Landscapes are generally best taken in early morning or late afternoon. Portraits are best when taken in soft light. Architecture requires hard, clean light and strong shadows. For almost all subjects I would emphasize that soft, diffused sunlight is generally more attractive than strong sunlight.

NOTES ON PLATES (pages 53-67)

53   YAP GIRL DANCING,
CAROLINE ISLANDS.

Rolleiflex, Tessar 75mm F3.5, 1/100 at f5.6, Anscochrome.

54-55   LINCOLN MEMORIAL,
WASHINGTON, D.C.

Deardorff 5 × 7, 120mm Aristostigmat F8, 15 seconds at f11, Harrison F3 filter, Ektachrome.

56-57   TETON RANGE.

Panon 120, 50mm Panon F2.8, 1/2 second at f16, Ektachrome.

58-59   BITS AND SPURS, PANHANDLE-
PLAINS HISTORICAL MUSEUM,
CANYON, TEXAS.

Deardorff 8 × 10, 12-inch Commercial Ektar, 1/2 second at f32, Ektachrome.

60-61   MIANGO GIRLS DANCING,
NIGERIA.

Canon VI, 50mm Canon F1.8, 1/50 at f2.8, Kodachrome.

62-63   CANOES AND TORCHLIGHT,
TAHITI.

Contax II, 50mm Sonnar F1.5, 1 second at f1.5, Kodachrome.

64   PALMS AND MOONLIGHT, SAMOA.

Contax II, 85mm Sonnar F2, 10 seconds at f2, Kodachrome.

65   FALLEN CHERRY BLOSSOM
PETALS, UENO PARK, TOKYO.

Canon VI, 35mm Canon F1.9, 1/30 at f5.6, Skylight filter, Kodachrome.

66-67   SHELBURNE MUSEUM, VERMONT.

Deardorff 5 × 7, 400mm Schneider Tele-magor F5.5, 1/25 at f11, Ektachrome.

◘ 4

SPECIAL EFFECTS

The aim of every serious photographer is to evolve a style that reflects his own taste and character. He arrives at this through his own experience, his successes and failures during experimental work, and by constant study of nature and everything else around him. Inevitably he will also be influenced by the style of other photographers, those he admires most, and by the paintings of artists who work along parallel lines.

My own efforts to be a painter have helped a great deal in the understanding of color, of its various applications and juxtapositions. In studio work the photographer is less limited. He can select different-colored objects and backgrounds and get still further variations through the use of colored lights and filters, but he cannot get all the nuances and subtleties that are possible when dealing with pigment. Nevertheless, many of the effects that are possible with the camera and color-controlled film are, more frequently than not, overlooked by the person who has never painted.

Commercial photographers are almost always limited by the subject and colors they are given to work with, but other photographers—those with sufficient means, and those who photograph in their spare time to satisfy a creative urge—can be pure artists. Edward Weston, Alfred Steiglitz, and Paul Strand, working in black and white, are classic examples of photographers who have put art first and worked entirely for their aesthetic beliefs and ideals.

The freedom I learned from painting made un-controlled color photography difficult for me to accept. It was hard, after doing anything I pleased with paints, to find myself up against an aesthetic barrier with the other medium. Use of Harrison filters, both the coral and blue series, gave greater scope for expression in color but not

69

enough. The successful use of the light-yellow filter, the K1, encouraged me further, but this addition to my working equipment was still not enough to give me the real freedom I was seeking. For the time being, however, I had to be satisfied with this much progress.

Then I found the Harrison coral filter useful in adding a muted effect to all colors that are present in a subject. This effect may be studied by placing a light coral gelatin over a color photograph or painting. The gelatin adds its hue to all the colors and succeeds in pulling them together. Since my general preference is for less rather than more color, for muted tones rather than bright ones, this filter assisted me considerably in elementary color control. Similar experiments with the yellow filter indicated that the muting of all colors took place except that yellows and colors containing yellow, such as green and orange, were enriched by its use.

The real turning point in my attempts to interpret color came in 1953 when I went to the South Seas. My assignment there was to illustrate some fiction and non-fiction stories for *Life*. Almost all the writing involved was of a creative rather than a documentary nature. Since the personal views of the writers were the primary qualities of the material, I came to the conclusion that any effect I achieved that was related to these writings was proper and useful. One of my major subjects in the South Seas was an overgrown beach jungle in Samoa which was to be used to illustrate a Robert Louis Stevenson text. I found the jungle foliage too dull in itself, so I viewed the scene through a light-green filter to see how it looked. I wanted to see if this small addition of color would produce a more interesting picture that was in keeping with the mood Stevenson played up in his text. I was satisfied that it did.

Another subject in the same essay, was the Fatua waterfall in Tahiti (page 73), which Pierre Loti's writing had made famous. In order to avoid the heat of the day, my guide led me on the climb to the top of the waterfall, far back in the mountains, well before dawn. This ascent over rocks and roots, under heavy branches and vines in the semi-light of pre-dawn, produced an atmosphere of mystery and enchantment that I had not encountered before in my short stay in Tahiti. When we reached the waterfall, daylight had arrived and the sense of mystery had passed. I knew from previous experience that pre-dawn photographed blue, and without hesitation I photographed the waterfall using a blue filter. For purposes of comparison, I also made some exposures without the filter, but found the results quite uninteresting.

The most complex attempt at color control and interpretation in this South Seas assignment was the picture shown on page 68. The text I was illustrating here was a piece from Herman Melville's *Typee*. Melville describes his reactions to the mischievous convolutions of girls dancing by moonlight. I decided to try this photograph in daylight with filter control rather than in artificial light at night. I placed the girls in a glade under some heavy trees, choosing a place where a red-blossoming tree showed in the background, and eliminating any possibility of sunlight's touching the dancers. I then tried different filters on the upper lens of a Rolleiflex (this was before I possessed any single-lens 35mm reflex cameras) and studied the different effects. What the eye sees through the filter is never exactly the same as the film records, but the approximation is close enough. I then made a series of tests with a selection of different filters and had the Ektachrome developed in Papeete by a local photographer to whom I had supplied a color-developing kit. After studying the results I decided to retake the subject with a pair of filters, the Harrison B½, a blue one, and the Harrison fog filter #5, a heavy diffusing disk. Together these attachments produced the misty moonlight effect. I underexposed the picture slightly in order to emphasize some deep shadows, again to suggest night.

Color control need not be as arbitrary or strong as in the preceding examples. Nor may it be as suitable. In a photo story I did on Nigerian independence I made use of some color control without distorting the physical appearance of the subject. A reporting job imposes greater 'limitations than the interpretation of literature. This does not mean that the reporter-photographer cannot select his subjects carefully; indeed he must. But a mechanical facsimile on color film might provide too dull a picture, and in some circumstances therefore the use of a filter is not only reasonable but necessary. I believe that the only criterion of proper color control is whether or not the result looks both interesting and real.

Two examples of color control in the Nigerian series of pictures are "Oil Palms" (page 74) and "Women Pounding Grain" (page 75), which face each other as they did when originally printed in *Life*. The photograph of the women was made at sunset. To avoid glare, I placed the camera so that the sun was hidden behind the tree in the middle of the picture. The light was warm in quality, but since the women and calabashes, as well as the grain, were in slight shadow, I used a light-yellow gelatin filter (05 Y) to produce the same warm color in this area of the picture as well. As I have mentioned, filters generally have their strongest effect in the lower-key portions of photographs.

The all-over effect of "Oil Palms" is green, relieved only by the brownish tint of the stream and the figure. I used the weakest green filter, 05G, which was not enough to contaminate the water, yet sufficient to build up the green in the palms, ferns, and vines. A heavier filter, the 10G, would have been too much. These color gelatins, called color compensating filters, come in 2-, 3-, and 4-inch squares in six degrees of strength (05, 10, 20, 30, 40, 50). A polarizing filter is sometimes necessary to eliminate glare in a picture, or to darken the sky on the horizon. But it can also tend to over-dramatize the sky and should be used with caution. It requires an exposure increase of four times.

The enthusiasm with which manufacturers have produced sharper and sharper lenses has not been matched by the reactions of some photographers. Even as far back as a hundred years ago artists such as Julia Margaret Cameron fought the soulless detail produced by the mechanically perfect camera and lens. This photographer had soft-focus lenses specially ground for her use. Today photographers are still searching for methods of eliminating the cold-blooded perfection which is so difficult to channel into truly personal expression. Several of these photographers are discussed in the final chapter of this book. One of them, Ernst Haas, made a specialty of blurred color photographs; another, Irving Penn, has used monochromatic effects as well as exaggerated grain through excessive enlargement to give his work individuality, while Gordon Parks uses multiple exposures.

Slightly out-of-focus exposures can be a most effective device. The photograph "Cherry Blossoms" (page 24) was purposely taken so that it would not have a single sharp line; the characteristic softness of the blossoms is stressed by the fuzziness. Blurred pictures produce a somewhat similar effect. The photograph of the African fetish head on page 25 demonstrates this technique. I manipulated the equipment to get a normal, sharp picture of the head, but I failed to get any message from the sharp image in the ground glass. It was too real, and somehow uninteresting. I decided then to try for a blurred image and kicked the tripod slightly during the time exposure. This smearing of the highlights and detail resulted in an unusual and more expressive picture.

The photograph "White Pigeons in a Mission Courtyard" (page 79) is another example of blur. Unlike the African head picture, in which either the object or the camera had to be intentionally moved during the exposure, the pigeons themselves were constantly moving. When photographing action, we have the choice of stopping this action by using a faster shutter speed or of representing a natural blur as seen by the eye. In this example, the exposure was short enough to capture some of the birds momentarily at rest and others in movement. Partial blur is a very useful device for indicating action.

For instance, a hand blurred as a pitcher throws a baseball will indicate speed and help convey the action of such a picture. The blur of a dancer's skirt will do the same thing. See pages 26-27.

Another way to achieve sharp focus in one area of the picture and blur in another is to smear Vaseline on one part of a piece of clear glass and hold the glass in front of the lens, placing the glass to achieve the blur in the desired area. It is also possible to do this with a piece of black gauze burned out in the middle for the sharp area. Care must be taken not to get the gauze (or the Vaseline) edges in sharp focus. Similar experiments in off-beat photography can be made with pieces of color filters held between sheets of glass.

The simple photograph of fast-running horses in sharp focus (pages 76-77) demonstrates that there is also beauty in the traditional stopped-action picture. Although blurred action photos have become increasingly popular, there is still room for the other kind, too. Double- and multiple-exposure pictures have many interesting possibilities. The double exposure of a piece of pink tape which directs an automation machine to cut a piece of brass (page 107) enabled me to combine the two most important elements of a subject into one close-up image. In another picture, "The Brubeck Quartet" (page 119), multiple exposure permitted me to fit the four musicians into a vertical composition instead of the usual horizontal shape used for this sort of subject. In addition, this technique enabled me to make a modern pictorial image in keeping with the advanced music played by Brubeck.

The photograph Gordon Parks took of Brooklyn Bridge (page 145) is a perfect example of the imaginative use of multiple exposure to transform an ordinary subject into a poetic image. H. Landshoff has done a similar thing by repeating the image itself in the well-known photographs he has taken of the New York skyline.

Once more I would like to express a word of caution about special effects. The photographer should know what the techniques he employs will produce and, more important still, he must decide if they are an improvement over the uncontrolled image. This does not mean he cannot experiment, indeed he must, if he is to explore the possibilities of his equipment to the full, but, having had sufficient experience in one or another technique, he should then use the utmost discrimination in choosing the one best suited to the given subject or situation. No one appreciates an off-beat photograph just because it is off-beat, but if the special effect heightens the drama, humor, romantic aspect, sense of speed, excitement, loneliness, or any other emotion the photographer wishes to project, then it has reason.

NOTES ON PLATES (pages 73-79)

73 BLUE WATERFALL,
    TAHITI.
    *Contax II, 35mm Biogon F2.8, 1/15 at
    f4, BIO filter, Kodachrome.*

74 OIL PALMS,
    NIGERIA.
    *Canon VI, 28mm Canon F3.5, 1/10 at
    f8, CC-G05 filter, Kodachrome.*

75 WOMEN POUNDING GRAIN,
    NIGERIA.
    *Canonflex, 50mm Canon F1.8, 1/50 at
    f5.6, CC-05 Y filter, Kodachrome.*

76-77 CALUMET YEARLINGS,
       LEXINGTON, KENTUCKY.
       *Canon VI, 50mm Canon F1.8, 1/125 at
       f5.6, Skylight filter, Kodachrome.*

78 CALUMET MORNING WORKOUT,
    FLORIDA.
    *Praktina, 180mm Sonnar F2.8, 1/50 at
    f4, Harrison F3 and CC-05M filters,
    Kodachrome.*

79 WHITE PIGEONS IN MISSION
    COURTYARD.
    *Deardorff 5 × 7, 240mm Symmar F6.8,
    1 second at f22, Skylight filter, Ekta-
    chrome.*

Opposite: MINUTEMAN STATUE,
LEXINGTON, MASSACHUSETTS.

*Plaubel Pico 5 × 7, 240mm Symmar
F6.8, 5 seconds at f11, Ektachrome.
Four lamps.*

◻ 5

LIGHTING

LOCATION LIGHTING

The technique of lighting is so complex and varied that I have thought it best to treat it in three separate sections. The first section deals entirely with location lighting, both interior and exterior; the second is devoted to studio lighting for still life; the third deals with lighting for portraiture.

The four most important standard kinds of photographic light are daylight, incandescent, flash, and stroboscopic (or "strobe"). Each of these has a different color temperature, which is measured scientifically in Kelvin degrees (commonly denoted with the letter K, which is the abbreviation I use here.) There are also variances within each type of lighting. Incandescent lamps, for example, are manufactured in different K degrees. Daylight, which is generally 5900K, varies a great deal, depending upon the time of day and the weather. The chart on page 155 lists the various types of light and their color temperatures.

The light we use may be direct or indirect. When the light from the sun or a lamp hits a subject directly and illuminates it, we have direct lighting. When the light is turned onto another object such as a wall or reflector and bounced to the subject, we have indirect or bounce lighting. The latter is understandably popular because the unapparent source of light results in pictures with a feeling of greater naturalness.

The making of photographs by whatever natural light happens to illumine a subject indoors is known as working with "available light." This technique is another very popular development with the younger photographers. Most of these men are concerned primarily with black-and-white photography, but the advent of new high-speed color films will undoubtedly encourage them to take more candid color pictures indoors as well. The same enlargement problem of coarse grain and lack of detail in high-speed black-and-white photography will pertain, except that with the use of color film a gray, rather muddy picture is likely to result. Until color is made in faster films, supplementary light such as floods or flash is usually needed for indoor subjects except for those that can be photographed by time exposure. However, it is sometimes possible with careful technique, especially bounce lighting, to photograph indoors without apparent recourse to artificial light. There are instances, such as in the crime pictures by Gordon Parks, where the poor quality of the color resulting from available light gives the photographs a greater sense of reality and drama.

Additional lighting is sometimes employed outdoors because of the inability of color film to register the wide range between highlight and shadow in one exposure. The film will not "stretch" as far as most fast black-and-white films do. Kodachrome has comparatively little latitude with subjects taken in bright sunshine; exposure for the highlights makes the shadows go black, and exposure for the shadows results in highlights that are pasty, especially in faces. In outdoor portraiture, professionals add illumination by reflecting the sunlight onto the dark areas of the picture, or by using blue flash bulbs balanced for daylight color film.

To bounce light, some sort of a reflector is used. I have employed white towels and bedsheets, pieces of white paper or cardboard, silver paper from enlarging-paper boxes, kitchen aluminum foil, ferrotype tins, mirrors, and any other handy objects that would reflect light without altering its color. On one occasion I used the camera's self-timer to make an exposure so that I could stand near the subject, allowing my white shirt to reflect additional light.

The best portable reflector I own is made up of four 16-x-20-inch white mounting boards. The back of each board is covered with slightly crumpled aluminum foil. (Crumpled foil lessens the hard edges of the reflected light.) These four boards are taped together to form a 30-x-40-inch reflector that can be folded at the seams for easy transport. I use the foil side for brighter reflection, and the white side for softer light.

The photograph of the bust of Andrew Jackson (page 85) was made outdoors so that the hickory trees Jackson had planted would show in the background. The sculpture was completely in shade, except for the back light seen at the right side of the statue. The face would have been too dark if the exposure had been made for the part touched by sunshine, too white and pasty if the exposure had been increased for the shadow side. Two mirrors were used as reflectors to obtain a balanced color exposure, one held to cast an even light over the entire face, the other placed on the left to lighten the trees

directly behind the head near the chin so that the characteristic bark of the shagbark hickory would register. This method produced a portrait-like quality in the bust which would not have been possible in natural daylight.

Another way to balance sunlight is to use flash. Manufacturers such as General Electric and Sylvania produce flash bulbs that have been dipped in blue dye so that the resulting light is similar to daylight. There are a great variety of strengths and sizes of bulbs, and most amateurs favor the peanut type. A table for the exposure index of the lamps is at the end of the book. It should be noted that when the lamp is used only as a fill to lighten a shadow area the normal exposure for the subject in sunlight is usually the correct one. If the subject is close and the lamp not diffused, some compensation should be made for the increased light from the lamp. I recommend that the lamp be covered with a thin white handkerchief or similar material, which must be arranged so that it does not touch the bulb itself and burn. White plastic diffusers are also available for the same purpose: these will soften the light and eliminate a second shadow. Some professionals use the spun-glass type of diffuser, and this diminishes the light about one stop. The kind of subject and the mood of the picture will dictate the proper amount of light and its position. However, care must always be taken not to use too much added light from one source, or it will produce an unnatural effect.

The portrait of President and Mrs. Truman in front of their home in Independence (page 95) required additional lighting. The exposure reading on the house itself, which is pure white, was at the top of the meter, which registered 1600 foot-candles. This meant that to expose the building properly the exposure would be a 1/25 of a second at F22 with 5 × 7 Ektachrome. The reading on the Trumans was 1/4 of a second at F22, an impossible range for color film in one exposure. For the purpose of filling in the shadows and bringing the exposure of both the Trumans and the house to 1/25 at F22, I used two blue G.E. #22's near the camera. The lights, diffused by a white handkerchief over each, had to be placed high on stands to avoid reflections in Mr. Truman's eyeglasses. The set-up was made approximately one hour before the five-minute sitting, and two other people of the same build were used as stand-ins. On important portrait assignments it is a good idea to take along a stand-in, if possible, so that the actual sitter can be spared the ordeal of preliminary testings of light, color, camera angle, etc., and appear fresh for the sitting itself. This is not to say that good photographs don't often occur after many pictures have been taken, but it does save time in getting the subject in a more relaxed frame of mind.

Blue flash bulbs can also be used to light up more than one area in an outdoor photograph. The shot of the Pyramide Restaurant in France (page 86) was made with four G.E. #50 blue lamps. In any language this is a lot of light. The bulbs, the largest ordinary flash bulbs made, emit their light over a longer period than the smaller kinds, and if all this light is to be used shutters must be set at 1/25 of a second or slower. To obtain the maximum amount of light I often do not synchronize these lamps exactly. For example, if a time exposure of a second is given, flashes can be set to go off during the long exposure. The arrangement of lamps for this photo is shown on page 150. Note that the two lamps in front are set as close to the lens as possible and are double-diffused in order to impart a soft, natural-light look to the food. Also, placing the lights next to the lens eliminated most shadows. The third light was set for the champagne bottle and sycamore tree behind it, and the fourth light, undiffused like the third, was set for the people at the table in the rear. It is interesting to note that even with all the lamps the background of lawn and flowers is a touch overexposed. This, however, has a quite natural and pleasing effect.

The same problem of illuminating dark areas occurs indoors when a view through a window is part of the photograph. "Tour d'Argent Restaurant, Paris" (page 87) posed the problem of photographing an elegant interior that showed a view of Paris through the large windows. This kind of photograph is one of the most difficult to make. The exposure for the outdoor scene must first be determined with the exposure meter; then enough light must be used on the indoor subject to match the outdoor exposure. In this instance, the exterior reading was 1/2 second at F32, and two #50 blues with single diffusers had to be used next to the camera to illuminate the interior area. The distance of the lamps from the subject and the compensation for the diffusers used can of course be computed to give the correct exposure. The new 4 × 5 Polaroid back for professional cameras now enables the photographer to test the exposure on polaroid film before he takes the color shot; a neutral-density filter on the lens can bring the polaroid film down to the same speed as the color emulsion. See page 154 for a table on these ratios.

Flashbulbs are rated in strength by the manufacturer, and the lamp wrapping always lists the recommended index for a particular film. If the lamp is rated at 50 for Kodachrome, for instance, you measure the distance between the lamp and the subject and divide that into 50 to obtain the correct F stop. A chart giving the information on these lamps, as well as strobe, is on page 154.

Another way to balance outdoor and indoor light is to use blue photofloods. Occasionally these lamps vary in color temperature, but they are satisfactory for general use. The photograph of the sculptor Chaim Gross (page 89), was made with two #2 blue photofloods set in polished aluminum reflectors. The overhead lamp in the picture was also fitted with a #2 blue so that the daylight quality of the light would be constant. This type of picture problem—large windows admitting daylight—requires the use of daylight film with either blue flash or flood. You cannot mix daylight and incandescent film and light unless you do so deliberately for some special effect. You may, of course, draw the blinds or curtains so that all the illumination is artificial, but in so doing you lose the atmosphere that a daylight view through the window gives.

To illustrate the opening story of *Life*'s food issue, on New York's appetite, I had to illuminate two enormous areas, the Washington Market and the Lincoln Tunnel ramp leading into New York. The ramp photograph (pages 92-93) was done by combining daylight and flash and making four separate exposures on the same piece of film. The camera was an 8 × 10 view fitted with a 12cm wide-angle lens, and daylight film and daylight bulbs were used. The first exposure was made for the outline of the ramp and the New York skyline in late afternoon; the time of exposure was about one-half normal, so that the scene would still look dark after the remaining exposures were made. The lens was opened again when the lights of New York came on, and this also caught the lights of the cars moving on the ramp. For the third exposure, trucks were placed in position on the ramp, traffic was stopped by police cars, and five men, each carrying a reflector with a #50 flash lamp pointed at the trucks, had their bulbs fired in unison by one man with connecting wires to each reflector. The lens was again closed until one truck could come right around and be flashed in the foreground for the fourth opening of the shutter. A walkie-talkie from the camera to the men with the flash bulbs and to the police cars coordinated the opening of the shutter with the action on the ramp.

Clear flash bulbs provide the most powerful light with the least amount of equipment. A special filter is recommended by the film manufacturer if the film is not balanced for clear flash but for 3200K incandescent lighting. The usual one used to transform flash into 3200K is the Eastman 81c. Care must be taken not to permit daylight to mix either with clear flash or 3200K incandescent light; otherwise a bluish tinge will result. Tables for the relative indexes of various flash bulbs in relation to types of color film are on page 154.

NOTES ON PLATES (pages 85-96)

85 BUST OF ANDREW JACKSON.

Plaubel Pico 5 × 7, 240mm Symmar F6.8, 1/2 second at F32, Skylight filter, Ektachrome.

86 PYRAMIDE RESTAURANT, VIENNE, FRANCE.

Deardorff 5 × 7, 180mm Symmar F6.8, 1 second at f22, Ektachrome. Four blue G.E. # 50 flash bulbs; see page 150 for lighting diagram.

87 TOUR D'ARGENT RESTAURANT, PARIS.

Deardorff 5 × 7, 135mm Ektar F4.7, 1/2 second at f32, Ektachrome. Two blue G.E. # 50 flash bulbs.

88 WILLIE HARTACK IN RACING SILKS, FLORIDA.

Canon V, 35mm Canon F1.9, 1/50 at f5.6, Kodachrome. Two Strobo-Research # 4 units and one Mightylight to low ceiling.

89 CHAIM GROSS IN HIS STUDIO.

Linhof 4 × 5, 127mm Ektar F4.7, 1 second at f8, Ektachrome. Three # 2 Daylight photofloods.

90 MEDICAL LECTURE, UNIVERSITY OF MEXICO.

Canon V, 28mm Canon F3.5, 1/50 at f5.6, Kodachrome. Four portable strobe units; see page 150 for diagram.

91 STAIRCASE SCENE AT MONTREAL MUSEUM BALL.

Deardorff 5 × 7, 120mm Aristostigmat F6.3, 1/50 at f22, Ektachrome. Twelve Ascor 800-watt seconds units; see page 151 for lighting diagram.

92-93 LINCOLN TUNNEL RAMP.

Deardorff 8 × 10, 120mm Aristostigmat F6.3. First exposure for ramp and skyline in late afternoon, 1/2 at f8; second exposure for car and city lights, 10 seconds at f8; flash exposure for trucks, 1/25 at f8, five # 50 bulbs; additional exposure for front truck, 1/25 at f8.

94 MRS. MARKEY'S AFTERNOON TEA.

Canon V, 35mm Canon F1.9, 1/12 at f2.8, Kodachrome A. Four portable reflector floods bounced from ceiling. No. 1 photofloods in table lamps.

95 PRESIDENT AND MRS. TRUMAN AT INDEPENDENCE, MISSOURI.

Deardorff 5 × 7, 180mm Symmar F6.8, 1/25 at f32, Ektachrome. Two diffused # 22 G.E. blue flash bulbs from above.

96 INDIAN COOKING.

Synar 8 × 10, 12-inch Commercial Ektar, 5 seconds at f45, Ektachrome. Bounce incandescent lighting to white walls and ceiling.

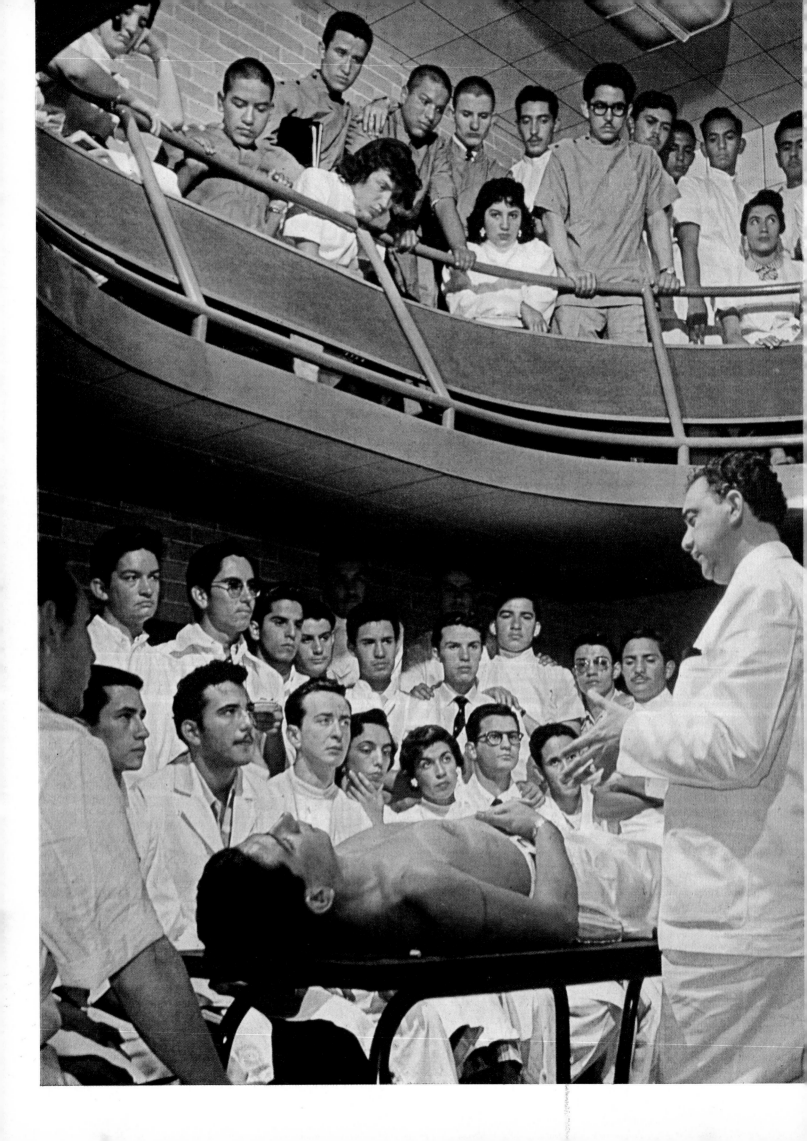

Stroboscopic light also provides daylight color lighting. A small strobe unit can easily be used to balance shadow parts of contrasting subjects. Strobe, too, is very useful for general photographic lighting. The photograph of Willie Hartack (page 88) is the result of bounce strobe lighting. Two medium-size units called SR 4's, which have an output of 400 lumen seconds (each unit is rated by the manufacturer), were placed at a height of about five feet so the beams would hit the ceiling over Hartack's head. This gave a soft, even light to the entire picture area and achieved a natural effect. Larger subjects, such as the medical lecture at the University of Mexico (page 90), required direct lighting from the same strobe units. The lighting chart for this picture is reproduced on page 150.

Incandescent lighting is also useful on location or in home photography. Lamps may be purchased which contain built-in reflectors for convenient portability. They are available in both flood and spot designs and come in a great variety of strengths. Some of these lamps, called photofloods, do not draw high current but produce high wattage. Their life span is shorter than the normal ones, and they have a different Kelvin rating in color temperature. Camera stores will give you the rating of any kind of bulb you buy.

The photograph of Mrs. Markey and her trainers (page 94) is an example of what can be done with small built-in reflector floods. Four lamps were directed at the low white ceiling to bounce the light back onto the various parts of the subject, the silver tea service, the three people, and the paintings on the wall. In addition, No. 1 photofloods were fitted into the three table lamps that appear in the photograph, adding light and giving a natural effect of interior illumination.

The use of floodlight outdoors is demonstrated in the picture of the minuteman statue (page 80). To avoid the ordinary daylight picture of this famous statue I followed the suggestion of *Life*'s Bernard Quint and waited until twilight when the sky became deep blue; then I illuminated both the tavern and the statue. I used a blue flood on the tavern to suggest moonlight and a clear #4 movie flood (a very large bulb with a Mogul base) near the statue so that it would photograph on the warm side. Then, to suggest candle and fireside light inside the tavern, I placed yellow gelatins over the lamps just inside the window.

People often ask me when to use flash, strobe, or incandescent light. Outdoors a small flash bulb is generally adequate for close-ups in which contrast must be controlled. Larger scenes require stronger bulbs. In most cases, diffusion on the flash is desirable. Strobes may substitute for flash, but this equipment is much more expensive; it is also much heavier and often requires a station wagon or truck to carry an adequate supply for a big assignment.

When definitive lighting is needed, the initial use of flash requires a photoflood guide lamp alongside the flash reflector. The guide lamp tells exactly what the lighting effect will be—an extremely important consideration in portraiture work. Strobes of the large type often contain a built-in pilot light, but these are generally too weak to serve as an effective guide. These lamps sometimes require a filter with daylight film.

The proper use of color-balanced incandescent illumination and film balanced for it is the most definitive type of controlled lighting indoors. Here the photographer can adjust his lights and measure them carefully with an exposure meter. In the field, clear flash bulbs used with the filter recommended in the box of film will give exact results without worry about voltage and lamp charges.

STILL LIFE

This section on lighting is addressed primarily to the studio photographer, to the photo-journalist who does studio-type pictures in the field, and to the advanced amateur who is interested in table-top photography.

In the early days of photography the major source of light in the studio came from a skylight. The light fluctuated with the time of day, and it also varied according to the weather and the season. In color photography, the skylight as a sole light source is particularly inadequate, and today two major lighting systems have taken its place: strobe and incandescent. Of the two systems, incandescent is the more commonly used. The major advantage of strobe is that it is powerful enough for action pictures to be taken in the studio; it also eliminates the necessity for models to hold still during the exposure. In the still-life field this is unimportant, and it is difficult to study lighting effects with strobe pilot lights.

Any type of incandescent studio lighting equipment may be used provided the color temperature of the bulbs is 3200K. These lamps are especially designed for color film. Studio equipment can be as elaborate and expensive as the situation permits. To take an extreme example, in the *Life* magazine studio a twenty-foot wall is completely hidden from view by the array of lamps. There are three 5000-watt units. One is a spotlight with a fresnel lens, which, with a movable lamp in front of the reflector, permits the narrowing or spreading of the light. This spotlight slides up and down a vertical metal stand and can be swung in any direction. There are two floods, each mounted on a long boom, and the direction of the lamp housing, up or down and side to side, is controlled by hand levers at a convenient height on the stand. There are several 2000-watt spotlights similar to the 5000-watt ones. Large batteries of floods are mounted on wheeled stands with height controls. The reflector housings of these floods are large enough for 1000-, 1500-, or 2000-watt lamps and have clips in front to hold diffusion disks or color gelatin attachments. There is also a group of small fresnel spotlights equipped with 750-watt bulbs, on small stands which are easy to wheel around a subject. Finally there is a variety of small spotlights, such as the inky-dinky (a tiny spot) and several small-size boom spots which are handy because they can easily be kept out of the way of the subject. Many of these lights are equipped with what are called barn doors. The barn-door attachment, on the front of the housing, consists of four metal leaves which, when partially closed, reduce the area illuminated by the light. Barn doors are also useful in preventing the light from hitting the camera lens.

Still-life lighting may be either direct or bounced. With the latter technique, as described before, unwanted shadows can be eliminated almost entirely. When several lamps are used directly on the subject, each light throws its own shadow, which often produces a confused and muddy-looking picture.

Shadowless lighting can also be achieved by surrounding the lens with lights. Marty Bauman, an advertising photographer, found it convenient to build a doughnut-shaped tin unit to encircle the lens. Into this unit he can fit a dozen No. 1 photofloods, spacing them evenly around it. Shooting through the center of this circle of light automatically eliminates all shadows in a picture; each light illuminates the shadow area cast by the next light in the circle, so that in the end no shadows exist. A double-diffused flood on each side of the lens will do almost the same thing. Then one strong direct light called the "key light" is manipulated to produce the main lighting effect, the diffused lights filling in the

shadows and giving an over-all balanced result. Some photographers use several strong lights in addition to the fills.

A convenient way of bounce-lighting still-life subjects is to surround the setting with movable walls of white paper. Sheets of white background paper can easily be attached to large wooden frames. If these frames are then set on rollers they can be maneuvered into position after the still-life and camera are set up. A white paper ceiling not too far from the subject is also important. Lights are then directed toward the ceiling and walls to reflect onto the subject. The photograph "Indian Cooking" (page 96) was made in this manner. However, the rather elaborate studio lighting used for this particular photograph could be simplified. A battery of inexpensive aluminum reflectors equipped with 500-watt 3200K lamps is adequate for most purposes. These reflectors can be mounted on strips and hung facing the white panels; others may be mounted along the sides or bottom. This will give a fine bounce light at very little cost.

I have developed a portable outfit for studio lighting which is contained in one large fiber case not too heavy for me to carry. The lamps are the 500-watt built-in reflector type, rated at 3200K. They screw into sockets on alligator clamps which can be attached to metal stands, a chair, a door, or any other handy object. There are eight lamps and eight sockets; four of the bulbs are flood and four are spot. In addition, the outfit includes a few tiny mushroom lamps which I use when less light is needed, barn doors for four of the lamps, a set of metal clips for attaching either diffusers or colored gelatins, a group of white board reflectors for bounce lighting, a few No. 1 photofloods to insert in home table lamps, some three-way sockets, extra extension wire, a special adapter to plug an extension into a light-bulb socket when there are no handy outlets, a screwdriver and pliers, and some fuses in case I overload the line and blow out the lights.

Another important piece of equipment is a small voltmeter with which to check the available voltage in an unknown location. Lamps are rated at 3200K for 110 to 120 volts current. If the voltage drops below 110 a change in color will take place. The Eastman #82 filter will correct the color change down to a voltage reading of 100. The #81 filter will do the same for readings above 120 and up to 130 volts. Most ordinary house lines will not take more than 1000 watts without blowing a fuse or dropping voltage, so care must be taken. A long extension wire can often be used to bring in current from another room which is on another line; thus additional light becomes available. The voltage of the line must be checked when all the lights are on. Different times of day will also affect the voltage; after nightfall, for instance, more current is being used.

One of the techniques in color photography requiring the utmost precision is the copying of paintings. "Girl with the Red Shoes" (page 105) was photographed on location with my portable outfit. To take such pictures, the painting first of all should be placed flat against the wall or exactly perpendicular and level on a stand. The camera must then be placed so that the height of the lens exactly corresponds to the center of the painting. To accomplish this the height of the painting must be measured, then half of this height added to the distance between the bottom of the painting and the floor; the camera is elevated until the center of the lens is at that height. The camera must then be manipulated until it faces the painting straight-on. A piece of string held from the lower right corner of the painting to the lower right corner of the camera should be equal in length to the corresponding measurement on the left side. The camera has to be moved until both sides are equal. If proper care is not taken the painting will be keystoned: one side of it will appear larger than the other in the photograph. This technique may sound more complicated than simply viewing the painting through the ground glass of the camera, but in actual fact it is the only possible way because we cannot rely upon getting exactly square results by eye alone.

As for lighting, the painting should be lit by either two lamps or four, depending on its size. The position of the lights must be far enough to the side to avoid reflections from the surface. An exposure meter should be used to determine that the illumination is equal over the entire area.

For photographing a painting for reproduction, there is an excellent device made by Kodak, called color-control patches, which will assist the engraver in color-correcting the printing plates, should this prove necessary. It is a strip of cardboard printed with a group of colors which can be placed next to the painting as you photograph. The engraver has a similar strip, and he can see if the blue or red or yellow is too strong or too weak in the photograph and make proper compensation when he does his color separations.

Some subjects, other than paintings, may look better if they are not photographed for accurate color. "Interior of a Jet Engine" (page 106) and "Pink Automation Tape and brass carving" (page 107) are two cases in point. The jet-engine interior had been painted in vivid colors by the engineers who used it as a demonstration model. There was so much color in the subject that I decided it

was not necessary to add colored light. In the other subject the opposite was true: neither the pink tape nor the piece of brass had enough color to make a dramatic picture. I decided to make a double-exposure photograph: the first exposure was on the tape, with a pink gelatin over the floodlight; the second illuminated the brass with yellow light. This produced two vivid images which were able to hold their own although partially superimposed over each other.

Color gelatins were also used in the photograph of the early American wooden bowls (page 104). In this case I covered the lights with yellow and orange gelatins to enrich the quality of the wood. This lighting also gave an attractive color quality to the white paper used as a background. Besides the gelatins, I used diffusers over the floods to soften the lighting.

"Benjamin Franklin's Printing Press" (page 101) was made with portable studio lighting in the Providence Museum. The background of the Almanac, which is an example of the journal printed by this press, was a photographic copy enlarged to mural size and shipped to the museum. The illumination was four reflector flood 500-watt 3200K lamps, and a very light-blue gelatin was used on two of the lamps to add color quality both to the old press and to the predominantly white background. I felt that this would provide more atmosphere than neutral lighting.

Shiny metals, such as silver and gold, must be photographed with reflected light. Direct lighting on metal produces a distracting small circle of brilliant light, which ruins the picture. The photograph of some examples from Yale University's silver collection (page 102) was made entirely with reflectors. The objects were surrounded by sheets of white paper and the brilliance of the silver was dependent on the amount of light bounced off the reflectors. Some photographers actually build a tent of white paper to enclose the objects and then cut a small hole in the front wall to insert the lens. Personally I prefer using scattered reflectors so that a few dark reflections can be created to stress the various shapes of the metal objects and give the photograph greater depth.

The elaborate photograph "Mrs. Markey's Trophies" (page 103) was taken outdoors with huge reflectors. Two twenty-foot panels ten feet wide were made with white background paper mounted on wooden frames. These were placed on either side of the camera to reflect light on each piece of gold and silver. White bed sheets were placed on the ground between the camera and trophies to throw light up onto the lower parts of the cups. The wooden panel on which the trophies were mounted faced north so that no direct light would hit them. The panel

NOTES ON PLATES (pages 101-108)

101 BENJAMIN FRANKLIN'S
PRINTING PRESS.
Deardorff 5 × 7, 180mm Symmar F6.8, 30 seconds at ƒ32, Ektachrome. Four portable RFL2 lamps, light blue gelatins on two lamps.

102 (a) EARLY AMERICAN SILVER,
YALE UNIVERSITY COLLECTION.
Deardorff 5 × 7, 180mm Symmar F6.8, 32 seconds at ƒ45, Ektachrome. Bounce lighting with six RFL2 lamps.

102 (b) SET-UP FOR PHOTOGRAPH
ON PAGE 103.

103 MRS. MARKEY'S TROPHIES.
Deardorff 5 × 7, 180mm Symmar F6.8, 1 second at ƒ22, Ektachrome, Skylight filter.

104 EARLY AMERICAN WOODEN
BOWLS, OLD STURBRIDGE,
MASSACHUSETTS.
Deardorff 5 × 7, 180mm Symmar F6.8, 30 seconds at ƒ45, Ektachrome. Three RFL2 lamps with orange gelatins on two lamps.

105 GIRL WITH THE RED SHOES,
DUPONT MUSEUM,
WINTERTHUR, DELAWARE.
Deardorff 5 × 7, 18cm Symmar F6.8, 20 seconds at ƒ16, Ektachrome. Four RFL2 lamps.

106 INTERIOR OF A JET ENGINE.
Deardorff 5 × 7, 120mm Aristostigmat F6.3, 2 seconds at ƒ22, Ektachrome. Two RFL2 lamps.

107 PINK AUTOMATION TAPE AND
BRASS CARVING.
Deardorff 8 × 10, 12-inch Commercial Ektar, pink tape exposed 2 seconds at ƒ11, brass carving 10 seconds at ƒ22, Ektachrome. Studio lighting.

108 PETER USTINOV AS KING LEAR.
Deardorff 5 × 7, 240mm Symmar F6.8, 1/50 at ƒ32, Ektachrome, Partial G10 filter, one lamp coupled to 12 Ascors.

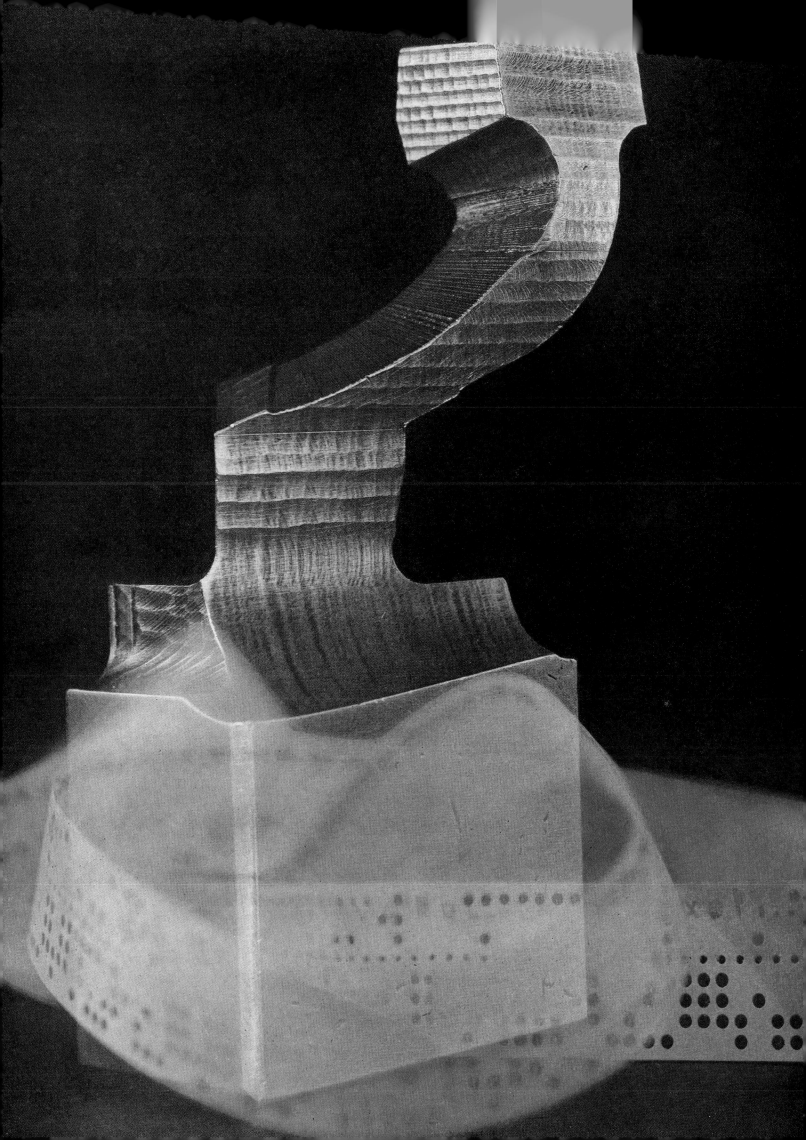

was designed to the exact proportions of a full page in *Life*, and sketches were made of the cup arrangements before the brackets to hold them were installed. The gold frame which sets off Mrs. Markey was rented in New York and expressed to Kentucky. The red with the blue stripe are the racing colors of Calumet, Mrs. Markey's stable; hence the choice of the blue backdrop behind Mrs. Markey. Her white dress was selected to tie in with the silver and thus keep the color scheme as simple as possible. It would have been possible to strip a separate portrait of Mrs. Markey into the frame, but this was not the way to achieve the natural result I wanted. A photograph showing the set-up for the trophy picture is reproduced on page 102.

Glass is another subject which should never, or almost never, be photographed with direct light. The most common technique is to backlight the glass with a diffused lamp. Another method is to place the glassware on thin glass shelves against a ground-glass background illuminated from behind. It is also possible to place the glassware on a sheet of ground glass and illuminate it from below. With this lighting, plus a little bounce lighting from above if needed, all shadows can be eliminated and excellent photographs achieved.

Sculpture photography at its best requires a knowledge of, and a feeling for, the sculpture itself. Each piece dictates its own special treatment. Some pieces require that much detail show; others look more effective if the roundness or form is stressed. Some pieces look well with certain shadow areas; others are better with none. My usual method is to place a diffused flood as near to the lens as possible. Another lamp of the same strength, but not diffused, is then moved around closer to the subject, until maximum roundness and sculptural quality of the object is achieved. This may require two lamps, one from each side. The amount of diffusion on the front lamp will determine the contrast between bright and shadow portions, and the amount of detail in the shadow. I generally use a white roll of paper for the background and pull the paper forward at the bottom so it curves gently onto the table and under the sculpture. The curved paper eliminates the horizon line. By placing the piece of sculpture several feet from the background, distracting shadows on the background can be eliminated. One or two or more lamps to illuminate the background are often useful in keeping it white. These lamps can also be used to light the back or top of the object to give it greater sculptural dimensions. There are over four hundred examples of sculptural lighting in my book *The Sculpture of Africa* (New York: Praeger, 1955), which may be of interest to photographers who make a specialty of this kind of work. See diagram page 150.

PORTRAITURE

Every photographer has his own approach to portraiture, and in the case of such well-known camera artists as Arnold Newman, Philippe Halsman, and Karsh each has such a characteristic style that his work is immediately identifiable.

Some of the problems every photographer has to face in portrait work are: deciding which aspect of the subject to dramatize, how to pose the subject, the relationship of the subject to the background, the facial expression, and the lighting. There are other imponderables which vary with each portrait.

Generally speaking, portraits are either candid in quality, such as the one of the jockey, Willie Hartack (page 88), or formal, such as the one of Audrey Hepburn (page 113). Both are portraits, yet they are very far apart in photographic and aesthetic treatment. Equally different are the portraits on pages 30 and 31. Sir Jacob Epstein, posed formally under one of his huge works, is looking steadfastly at the camera and appears as solid as his sculptures. By way of contrast, Morris Graves is gazing off in an almost furtive manner, his expression as elusive as his fragile paintings.

Other portraits in this book further demonstrate fundamental differences in the use of background and the degree of close-up. In the picture of President and Mrs. Truman in front of their Independence home, (page 95) the background has again been kept sharp because the building was important to the theme. Completely different is the photograph of Hermione Gingold (page 41), a classic example of a large head with almost no background. Whatever does appear behind the subject is out-of-focus and dimly lit.

Large head images made with long-focal-length lenses are often the best approach to a simple portrait. The long lens allows the photographer to get farther away from the subject, thus eliminating distortion and giving the lens a better chance to see around the head. The short depth of focus of the long lens throws distracting background detail into a soft blur and prevents ugly and distracting juxtapositions.

The photograph of Peter Ustinov playing the mad King Lear (page 108) is another example of the large head in portraiture. Here the facial expression and unusual make-up were emphasized so that the picture would be in keeping with the spirit of Ustinov's portrayal. He was actually screaming when the picture was made. The lighting was kept very simple. One very powerful strobe, placed a little above and to one side of the actor's head, was connected to twelve Ascor units which gave a tremendous wallop of close-up light. The strobe was used so that the shutter speed of the camera would be fast enough to stop the action of his screaming mouth. The wild mood, both of the actor and the picture itself, was augmented by dropping oak leaves into a wind machine which had been set just a few feet from Mr. Ustinov's face. This idea was prompted by the action of the play itself in the scene where King Lear goes mad on a wild, wind-driven heath. The weird effect was still further heightened by an unusual use of color filters. A four-inch square of Eastman G10, a moderate-green filter, was cut into several pieces; these were sandwiched between two pieces of clear glass and placed in front of the lens at a distance where their edges would be slightly out of focus. The green was arranged predominantly at the corners of the glass frame so that most of the actor's face would remain pink. In this way color was added only to parts of the picture.

A very different and conventional approach to portraiture is shown in the picture of Audrey Hepburn (page 113), who played the lovely young princess in the film *Roman Holiday*. The background used here is a black-and-white mural enlargement of a Roman arch. Miss Hepburn's demure expression and pose suggested using soft floodlights to bathe her in flattering light. A light-blue gelatin was used on one of the lights near the camera to emphasize the slight blue of her costume, the shadows on her face, and to repeat the blue lighting directed onto the background. Whereas Peter Ustinov was photographed with a sharp, critically focused lens, Audrey Hepburn's picture was done with a slight diffusion disk to convey her slightness and delicacy. Direct strobe on her would have been brutal.

Bounced lighting can achieve the kind of softness that is most often desirable in portraits of women. The picture of Gwen Verdon (page 114) playing a harlequin was made with bounce strobe. After Miss Verdon was posed, large aluminum-foil-covered flats were wheeled

into position on both sides of her, and two smaller ones were placed on each side of the camera. The ceiling was a special white panel suspended about six feet over Miss Verdon's head. Twenty-four Ascor units were then evenly distributed over the entire area to bounce light back to Miss Verdon. Strobe was chosen because part of her action was to drop the inside part of the confetti roll she was holding in her eye like a monocle. As can be seen from the picture, the paper was in the process of unrolling just when the lens opened. No colored light was used because I wanted to preserve the whiteness and simplicity of Miss Verdon's make-up.

The picture of Tyrone Power playing "Him" (page 115) was designed to portray the fractured hero of this modern play by E. E. Cummings. A mirror was broken and then loosely glued together so that the reflected image would be distorted and fragmented, in keeping symbolically with the character the author had created. The lighting was entirely spotlight for two reasons; first, the sharp image produced by this type of light added to the over-all effect, and second, it was essential that no light be reflected in any of the fractured areas of the mirror. Colored flats were set up to reflect in the mirror as well as in the broken image of Mr. Power's face.

Two portraits have been deliberately placed on facing pages to demonstrate the effect of one predominating color upon another. The page of Virginia Mayo (page 116) appears greener when seen together with the red image of Cyd Charisse (page 117). If the reader will cover one page he will notice that the lack of color contrast mutes the effect.

The portrait of Cyd Charisse, playing the lead in the musical film *The Band Wagon*, was made red-tinted with colored fill-in light directed on her. In addition, red gelatins were placed over the background lights to emphasize further the violent .mood of this particular sequence, which spoofed the sex-and-sadism craze in cheap paperback books.

The three portraits of Virginia Mayo are a demonstration of how to change the appearance of a subject through the use of colored light. The portrait at left of page 116 was made without gelatins. For the upper-right picture a light-green gelatin was used over one soft flood near the camera; the key light was kept pure. The lower-right portrait was made with a very light-green gelatin on the key light and stronger green gelatins on all the floods. Which of these three effects is best depends entirely on the judgment of the photographer as to the desired meaning of the portrait.

This concept, the choice of color to assist in the portrayal of character, is exemplified in the close-up of

Louis Armstrong (page 118). The portrait was part of a story in *Life* of my impressions of jazz. To me Louis Armstrong symbolizes the simple, direct, passionate approach to jazz, full of vigor, spirit, and even violence. Since I regard this portrait as one of my best I would like to dwell on the approach and technique it involved.

I began in New York by making a close-up drawing of a trumpet and then sketching in a portion of Armstrong's head, just showing above the brass. I knew Louis Armstrong always carried a white handkerchief in his left hand, and this I drew in to frame the edge of the trumpet. At the time I wanted to photograph the band leader, he happened to be on a cross-country tour, and his first two-day stop was in Tulsa, Oklahoma. I arranged to fly there and rented a large hotel room, taking with me a 5 × 7 Deardorff view camera, some lenses, film, four flash extensions, some colored gelatins, and a carton of clear G.E. #50 flash bulbs. I also shipped ahead of me a roll of black paper, to use for the background. Barbara Tompkins, who once worked on *Life* and was at the moment living in Tulsa, arranged for the sitting, and after Armstrong had arrived and taken his pose I discovered that his white shirt cuffs added more white to the picture than I had visualized when making my drawings. When I asked Louis to push them back he removed his jacket and tore out both sleeves before I could stop him. He said that shirts were cheap compared to the expense of my trip all the way from New York. The rest was simple. To make the exposure I used two flash bulbs, one from each side, and one with an orange gelatin. An 81c filter was used on the camera as recommended for flash by the film manufacturer. A short-focal-length lens was used in order to distort the size of the bell of the trumpet.

The treatment of the Brubeck Quartet (page 119), photographed for the same jazz story, is as different from the Armstrong picture as I was capable of making it. Both men are great musicians, but there the similarity between them ends. Brubeck is one of the leading exponents of progressive jazz, and the pictorial image I thought of for him in relation to the kind of music he played was as complex as a Picasso painting. To achieve an ultra-modern effect, five exposures were made on one film—one for each member of the quartet and two for Brubeck. The photograph was made in the *Life* studio with large strobe equipment while the men were actually playing. Each man's position was traced with red grease pencil on the ground glass to determine where each one registered and where each exposure would overlap. Overlaps were necessary to pull the images together and avoid the look of a paste-up. Different-colored gelatins were used on different members of the quartet to produce varying images. The saxophone was kept almost clean of color to add color contrast to the picture. One exposure of Brubeck was made with light-green gelatins: the second exposure, made without color, was added to suggest the constant turning of his head from side to side as he plays.

The last photograph in this chapter, "Roddy Mac-Dowell as Ariel" (page 120), is the most complicated portrait I have ever attempted. Mr. MacDowell was responsible for his own extraordinary make-up. Although it would appear from his picture that the background was at a minimum, it was very elaborate. Jean and Bill Eckhart, Broadway set and costume designers, did the costumes and decor of the entire "Dream Roles" story in *Life* of which this portrait formed a part. In *The Tempest* the spirit Ariel is supposed to be floating in space, and to produce this feeling Mr. MacDowell was placed behind a thin layer of theatrical gauze called scrim. Spangles and rhinestones were glued to this material and appear as the bright out-of-focus blobs seen in the foreground. The scrim was close to the camera to register out of focus and diffuse the image. Behind the head two more layers of scrim were hung about six feet apart. They too had jewels and spangles glued at random over their surface and can be seen dimly in the background. Both the scrims and MacDowell's head were illuminated with incandescent light. The scrims were in different shades of blue and green, enhanced by the use of blue and green gelatins over the floods that lit them. A light-blue filter over the camera lens helped pull all the colors together, muting the large assortment of spangles and jewels on Mr. Mac-Dowell's neck and shoulder. In addition to the blue filter, I also used a medium fog filter to soften the lines and hide the edge of the white bathing cap which concealed Mr. MacDowell's hair and was painted like the rest of his face. The photograph was purposely given a long exposure so that any slight movement of the actor would add softness and mystery to the image. Note the moved reflection of a light in the pupil of his right eye.

From all the foregoing it would seem that if there is such a thing as a general rule in portraiture, it is to know *who* is your subject and why *you* are photographing him, and then to use any photographic technique that will produce the particular result you want.

NOTES ON PLATES (pages 113-119)

113 AUDREY HEPBURN IN
Roman Holiday.
*Deardorff 5 × 7, 240mm Symmar F6.8,
1/10 at f8, Ektachrome. Studio lighting.
Two large floods, fill light with blue
gelatin on Miss H., one blue light on
background.*

114 GWEN VERDON AS HARLEQUIN.
*Deardorff 5 × 7, 240mm Symmar F6.8,
1/100 at f32, Ektachrome. Bounce studio
strobes.*

115 TYRONE POWER AS
E. E. CUMMINGS' "HIM."
*Deardorff 5 × 7, 240mm Symmar F6.8,
1/2 second at f16, Ektachrome. Studio
spotlights.*

116 VIRGINIA MAYO
(THREE PORTRAITS).
*Deardorff 5 × 7, 240mm Symmar F6.8,
1/10 at f11, Ektachrome. Studio lighting,
green gelatins added to lights. See chart
on page 151.*

117 CYD CHARISSE IN Bandwagon.
*Deardorff 5 × 7, 150mm Tessar F4.5,
1/5 at f16, Ektachrome. Studio lighting.*

118 LOUIS ARMSTRONG.
*Deardorff 5 × 7, 150mm Tessar F4.5,
1/25 at f22, Ektachrome. B. Two # 50
clear flash bulbs, yellow and orange gelatins, 81c filter.*

119 THE BRUBECK QUARTET.
*Deardorff 5 × 7, 180mm Symmar F6.8,
1/25 at f22, Ektachrome for each of five
exposures. Studio strobe equipment, colored gelatins.*

Opposite: RODDY MACDOWALL
AS ARIEL.

Deardorff 5 × 7, 240mm Schneider Sym-
mar F6.8, 1 second at f11, Harrison
B 1/8 filter and F3, Ektachrome. Studio
lighting.

◼ 6

COMPOSITION

Color composition—and this applies both to photography and painting—is always a question of design, the arrangement of masses and lines within a given area to produce an effect. This choice of effect must be dictated by the purpose of the picture. If serenity, for example, is the goal, the elements in the picture must be perfectly balanced and produce a quiet, restful composition. If a dynamic approach is the aim, diagonal lines and unequal masses are needed to set up action in the composition. The old rules that the sky must make one-third of the composition, or that the top of the picture must never cut a piece off a head in a portrait, are broken continually. Photography, in fact, helped change the classic rules of composition when painters fell in love with the accidental compositions produced in snapshots. Degas, for example, who was an avid amateur photographer, cut ballet girls in half at the edge of his photographs, or even at the top,

and as a result did the same thing in his paintings. I don't have documentary evidence of this, but any photographer studying Degas' ballet-rehearsal paintings will be immediately struck by their photographic cropping, especially at the edges. Another painter influenced in this way was Toulouse-Lautrec.

If we suggest that classic composition has been displaced—and I know this will be confusing, because it has not been—what is the photograph to emulate? First of all, classic composition is still a good beginning for any artist. You should know the rules before you break them. I believe that most of the photographs reproduced in this volume are founded on classic style. For example, the portrait of Audrey Hepburn (page 113) is typical of classic portrait composition: some space at the top of the head and more room on the side to which she is looking. Her head is against a dark mass of the arch but still breaking into it and combining with it to connect her with the background. In contrast, the portrait of Roddy Mac-Dowall (page 120) is cropped much closer and almost comes out of the frame. This is modern portraiture composition. The one of Tyrone Power (page 115) has the top of the head cut off. The native from New Guinea (page 18) is again tightly framed to dramatize the fierce make-up. In contrast, the Nigerian picture on page 19 takes in several other masked dancers besides the World War I gas mask, even though that, the most interesting part of the picture, is placed at the extreme left in order to create an additional pictorial excitement; placement in the center would have been too well balanced and dull.

Composition for color is an important consideration. In the picture of the Nigerian father and child (page 21), the design of the whole is pure and classical, but one strand of bright green in an almost monochromatic picture produces an interesting color composition. The Nara Pond picture (page 20) is again a meaningful example of poverty of color; the green of the weeping-willow leaves is important against the dull water. If this picture had been made on a sunny day with a blue-sky background, you would never have seen the tender spring leaves.

Another example of poverty or simplicity of color is the picture of the white horse (page 29), wherein the green is the only color and the shapes of the ferns in the foreground repeat almost exactly the ripples in the water being made by the wading horse. The picture of becalmed sailboats (page 43) is again almost monochromatic. So is the sand fence on Cape Cod (page 42). The Lincoln Memorial (page 54-55) is all blue, and the Oregon Coast (pages 34-35) almost all blue. A small bit of color can be very meaningful; in the picture of Ueno Park in Tokyo (page 65) where the cherry-blossom petals have been driven to the ground by the rain, the only color is the one purple raincoat seen through the lanterns.

Two photographs of bridges by Emil Schulthess and Gordon Parks (pages 144 and 145) demonstrate the extreme range of creative color photography. Schulthess's picture is straightforward photography, using an extreme telephoto lens to bring the setting sun close to the silhouetted framework of the bridge. It is the size of the sun that makes this real photograph seem unreal. Parks, in contrast, has used the Brooklyn Bridge as a subject for completely free pictorial expression, double- or triple-exposing the bridge until it becomes an imaginative fantasy. These pictures of bridges, both magnificent color photographs, were taken from radically opposed approaches.

◼ 7

EQUIPMENT
AND TECHNIQUES

CAMERAS

Every photographer, amateur and professional, is faced
with the problem of which camera to buy. If he purchases
more than one type (many people do) the problem is
further complicated by knowing which one to use for a
specific photograph. New camera developments in recent
years have compounded the problem. No sooner do you
choose and purchase a camera than the same manufacturer, or a rival, will come out with a new model which
he claims to be better. It is almost impossible, unless
money is no problem, to keep up with every change.
Trading in older models is very expensive, since it nearly
always brings you less than half of what you paid. But to
look at it another way, if great photographs have been
made in the past with old cameras, they can be made
with old models today, provided, of course, they are still
in good working condition. New equipment is not a
prime requisite.

I have often been asked at camera clubs which is my
favorite camera. This is difficult to answer because so
much depends upon the kind of photograph I wish to
take. Different cameras are made for different jobs. However, if I could own only one type of camera, my choice
would be the 35mm single-lens reflex. This is somewhat
surprising, since I began professional photography with a
studio 8 × 10 view camera. If I had to, I suppose I could
manage without my 5 × 7 view camera, with which I do
a good deal of work, or without my 4 × 5 Linhof, which
I take into the field, but I certainly could not do without
the 35mm camera. Whereas it is always possible to do
careful set-ups with the 35mm, it is impossible to make
candid or quick photographs with a view camera.

The 35mm cameras offer many advantages. They are
precision-made, they are all metal and rarely break down,
they are small enough to be carried everywhere, they are

easy to operate, they may be fitted with a variety of lenses of extreme focal lengths; it is possible to go from a 21mm wide angle to a 2000mm telephoto. In addition, 35mm film comes in a greater variety of emulsions, both color and black-and-white, than any other size. The smallest still camera, except for some tiny "spy" cameras which employ movie films, which will take Kodachrome is the 35mm. Kodachrome is still the most popular color film made, and for good reason.

Until single-lens reflex cameras were refined, I was perfectly content with the 35mm rangefinder camera. I now find that I use the reflex so much more than the rangefinder that it would be entirely feasible to eliminate the latter.

There are several cogent reasons for my preference of the reflex over the rangefinder in 35mm photography. The primary one is a matter of aesthetics, since technically both are equally good. In the rangefinder camera, the photographer looks at the image he intends to photograph through an optical viewfinder. The clean, sharp image merely defines the field of view; otherwise it is cold and lifeless and gives little impression of how the photograph will look. In contrast, the single-lens reflex permits the photographer to see the subject optically, with all the perspective, sharpness, and mood that the lens captures. The actual image seen in the viewfinder thus becomes a living thing. In addition, the problem of parallax is eliminated because there is no discrepancy between the lens and finder. With the single-lens reflex the photographer also has the opportunity of choosing the depth of focus, since the lens may be stopped down while he studies the effects of different depths.

There are twenty or so 35mm color illustrations in this book, many of them produced before the advent of the modern single-lens reflex camera. Although the German Exakta has been in existence for many years it lacked ease of handling for photo-journalism. Today the addition of the Swiss Alpha to the Japanese Canonflex, Nikon F, and Pentax gives the photographer a good choice in this field.

As I mentioned earlier, one of the great features of 35mm photography is its ease of handling. It is possible for the photographer to use his equipment almost as effortlessly as he writes or types. It was my habit when I was a war photographer to carry two Contax II's constantly around my neck. One camera was fitted with a 35mm F2.8 Biogon lens which, set at about 15 feet, was in focus from 8 feet to infinity at F8. The shutter speed was adjusted to the prevailing light. This meant that I had a camera ready to photograph anything almost as fast as I saw it. It was never necessary to check the settings; all

I did was simply pick up the camera and shoot. The other camera was fitted with a 135mm telephoto lens, which meant it had to be focused each time except for an infinity shot, such as one of a dive bomber.

The habit of having one camera completely ready for shooting has never left me. Had the camera not been pre-set I could never have taken the photograph of the white horse shown on page 29. To get the horse while it was still crossing the stream I jumped out of a car while it was still moving and took photographs as I ran back toward the animal. In the end I was fortunate in getting as many as four exposures. The first two pictures were poorly framed but the one I have reproduced was made after I had noticed (and utilized) the beautiful ferns that show in the foreground.

Another photograph made almost the same way is the one of the yearlings at the Calumet Farm in Kentucky (pages 76-77). When the reporter and I arrived at this spot by car I noticed that the horses were nervous. When I tried to approach them they started to run; however, I just managed to get close to the fence and shoot over it before they were gone. Again the camera had been pre-set. To keep the camera at the ready, I make it a practice to check prevailing light conditions throughout the day.

There are five photographs in this book from the Nigerian series published by Life in 1960. Like the other nine pictures that ran with the story, they were made with 35mm cameras exclusively. I carried two Canon vi cameras and two Canonflexes. The Canons were fitted with 28mm, 35mm, and 50mm lenses, the Canonflexes with 50mm, 85mm, 135mm, and 200mm. At the time I actually took the Nigerian pictures, which was a year before they were published, the Canon company unfortunately had not yet manufactured wide-angle lenses for their reflex camera. Three of the five pictures were made with the reflex: the father with his daughter (page 21), the backs of the girl dancers (pages 60-61), and the women pounding grain (page 75). It was especially useful in the case of the father and child to be able to study the degree of sharpness in the background and its effect upon the principal subject. In the photograph of the women pounding grain the sharpness of the calabashes in the foreground could be observed as well as the effect the warm sun had on the principal subjects. The girls' backs could have been photographed equally well with a rangefinder camera, but it was helpful to compose the group exactly through the lens.

"Oil Palms" (page 74) presented a hemmed-in situation requiring a wide-angle lens as well as increased depth of focus for over-all sharpness. The picture of the masked figures (page 19) was made with very little cooperation from the subjects. Realizing that this was likely to be the case and, knowing the extreme rapidity with which the Canon VI can be operated, I chose this camera for the job.

The picture of the double cherry blossoms on page 24 could not have been made without a reflex or ground-glass camera. The degree of softness and lack of depth of focus is what makes this photograph. Without the ground glass it would have been impossible to check the exact relationship of the blossoms and make such an interesting composition.

The $2\frac{1}{4} \times 2\frac{1}{4}$ single-lens reflex is also a very popular camera. The Swedish Hasselblad and the Japanese Bronica can both be highly recommended. Some of the advantages of the 35mm single-lens reflex camera are to be found in this larger type which, in addition, features interchangeable film backs. The disadvantages are the heavier camera and lens, the lack of ease in handling, the square format, and inability to employ Kodachrome film advantageously. Three photographs in this book were made with a Rolleiflex, before the advent of these newer designs. "Girls Dancing by Moonlight" (page 68) was taken with the "Rollei" so that I could first experiment with a few filters. By placing a filter on the upper lens of the Rollei it is possible to see the effect before switching the same filter to the taking lens below. This rather cumbersome process can be eliminated with the single-lens reflex. The same thing occurred with "Girl on Bridge, Paris" (page 46), where again I wanted to see the filter effect on the ground glass. The third Rollei picture —"Yap Girl Dancing" (page 53)—was made with this camera so that I could use Ektachrome instead of Kodachrome and get a less contrasty picture. I did not want the heavy blue sky and brilliant color that is identified with Kodachrome on a subject that was almost too colorful to begin with. Ektachrome at that time was not available in 35mm. Today all color emulsions are available in this size. The coarser grain of Ektachrome made the larger film size more suitable for reproduction.

From my point of view the disadvantage of the Rolleiflex and other twin-lens reflex cameras is the limitation of lens choice. Although a new model has been developed with several telephoto lenses, it is still not possible to employ anything shorter than normal focal length. Also, the square format is for me a very difficult area to compose. Many photographers who disagree with me on this point say the square image is desirable because with it the photographer may choose between a vertical and horizontal picture in the darkroom, or can adjust the shape by cropping the print. However, I find that many good photographers tend to make square pictures because they compose the picture exactly in the ground glass and then find that cropping the print spoils it. There is nothing wrong with a square image, but when photos are to be reproduced in a book or magazine, the proportions of the page usually call for a vertical or horizontal picture. This problem does not, of course, affect the amateur. Another feature of twin-lens reflex cameras which I don't much care for is that they are basically constructed so that you must look down into the camera while shooting. There are adjustments which allow eye-level finding, but these are not paramount in the design. Waist-level shooting has some advantages; for instance, one can thus sneak pictures without seeming to look at the subject—a technique I have often found extremely useful. But, generally speaking, looking down into the camera seems to give the photographer less contact with the subject. Finally, the effective aperture of the lenses for this size are not as fast as those made especially for the 35mm camera, and speed can be essential in some situations. However, I must add a kind word by mentioning that both Irving Penn and Bert Stern have made many of their superb photographs with $2\frac{1}{4} \times 2\frac{1}{4}$ twin- and single-lens reflex cameras. This only shows that the selection of a camera is very much a matter of personal preference, besides being dependent upon the type of photography for which it is needed.

Almost every camera type has a champion who is well able to demonstrate the usefulness and suitability of his choice. The $2\frac{1}{4} \times 3\frac{1}{4}$ Linhof, which is a cross between hand-held and view cameras, is the personal pride of Dmitri Kessel, one of our best photographers today. Mr. Kessel is equally at home with 35mm and large-view cameras but he finds that he does more and more of his *Life* assignments with the Linhof. The camera has many excellent features. It is well built, contains at least a double bellows extension, permits ground-glass focusing and viewing, and has some camera adjustments akin to those of a view camera. In addition to cut-film holders and film-pack adapters, the camera may be fitted with different roll-film holders. For instance, the 120 holder permits either 12 exposures of $2\frac{1}{4} \times 2\frac{1}{4}$ size or eight exposures of the $2\frac{1}{4} \times 3\frac{1}{4}$ format. A new size giving ten exposures with framing that enlarges perfectly to 8 × 10 is a recent development. For 35mm Kodachrome, yet another adapter is available. This is as wide a diversification of film materials as is possible with any single camera. The Linhof is not too large to prohibit hand-held photography, although it is far from being a candid camera. The rangefinder permits fast focusing, and there is a choice of specially built lenses that are exceedingly fine and very fast in aperture.

The Linhof has always been a favorite camera with magazine photographers, as the Speed Graphic has been with newspaper men. The 4 × 5 Linhof Technika has all the features of the 2¼ × 3¼ Linhof and a few improvements. Its body, however, is too large to accommodate the 2¼ × 2¼ film size practically. It can be done, but it is rather like using a rifle to fire a pistol bullet. The camera is small enough to carry almost anywhere and definitive enough in camera movements to accomplish almost any photographic assignment. It has a new type of brilliant finder with varying masks for each lens, which, with the coupled rangefinder, permit its use hand-held. I do not recommend this, however, except to steel-wristed people. An example of its use, on the tripod, is demonstrated in the photograph of Abu Simbel (page 32).

When in 1947 I photographed the Nile from its source to the sea, it would have been very difficult to carry around the usual view camera. Instead I worked with 35mm, Rolleiflex, and a 4 × 5 Linhof, with a large battery of lenses. Because the detail of the huge statue of Abu Simbel was important, the 4 × 5 camera was the logical choice for this photograph. The same was true of the subject on the facing page, taken inside a tomb. The Linhof can be opened and set up a good deal more quickly than the ordinary view camera and is also a sturdier. It was equally useful during my Atlantic Coast assignment where pictures had to be made near the sea in all kinds of weather. The pictures of the sand fence on page 42 and of the sailboats on page 43 were both made with the Linhof 4 × 5.

View cameras in general belong in the studio, although even there some of the photographs I have made with either the Linhof or a 5 × 7 view camera could have been accomplished with 35mm. David Douglas Duncan, who made the unforgettable photographs of the gaunt Marines in Korea with his Leica, a logical choice, also achieved an equally great but to me illogical success when he photographed the treasures of the Kremlin with the same 35mm camera. Not everyone agrees that this is an odd choice for the purpose, least of all Mr. Duncan; nevertheless, I could never advise anyone to try to do as he did. I believe the view camera is necessary for photographing paintings and other art objects of that nature.

The major advantages of the larger-view camera are obvious. It is a precise machine allowing maximum control and guidance from the operator. Distortions may be created or eliminated. The photographer has a large ground glass, either 5 × 7 or 8 × 10, in which to view the subject as the lens sees it; this enables the most careful composition possible. Even the use of the traditional black cloth over the operator's head assists the photographer in eliminating everything but the subject he is photographing. The larger film offers the opportunity of maximum rendition of detail and produces an image large enough to be seen without projection. The rising front enables the operator to keep the vertical lines straight when photographing architecture. Nothing is more disturbing than undeliberately tilted buildings or walls.

Two photographs in my story on Mrs. Markey's racing stable illustrate the comparative merits of the 35mm and 5 × 7 camera. In photographing Mrs. Markey at home, sitting with her two trainers in front of a group of paintings of Calumet Derby winners (page 94) it would have been illogical to use the 5 × 7 camera. The shot was made during a tea party for the entire staff and it would have been impossible to set up a view camera in the middle of the room without interfering with the party itself. What I wanted was a warm personal picture of Mrs. Markey and her companions. Whereas the use of the view camera would have necessitated long posed exposures and general freezing on the part of everyone concerned, the 35mm camera and use of bounce flood lighting (to which the group soon became accustomed) made it possible for me to take candid pictures in a friendly and relaxed atmosphere.

A very different problem existed when I set out to photograph Mrs. Markey and her trophies (page 103). It took two days before I was satisfied with every detail of the arrangement. The composition of the cups had to be seen in the large 5 × 7 ground glass, the reflections in each had to be controlled, and it was important to obtain enough detail in the cups so that each one would be recognizable in the photograph.

Another example of the proper use of the large-view camera, in this case an 8 × 10, is demonstrated by "Bits and Spurs" (pages 58-59). This picture required a maximum-size ground glass to encompass all the objects and to see each one of them clearly. Without as much detail the picture would have been flat and practically meaningless. The 8 × 10 view camera was also used in the photograph of New York taken from the Lincoln Tunnel approach (pages 92-93). Here again a large ground glass was needed to observe the whole subject in sufficient detail. I also had to use an extreme wide-angle lens designed for a smaller camera.

There are many view cameras on the market today, most of them suitable for a great variety of work. The best American view camera is made by Deardorff. One of the features of this camera is its ability to fold up compactly. Although I still own a 4 × 5 model, it is not my favorite view camera. I now operate a 5 × 7 Plaubel Pico, which racks along a single rail, and I like this better than the usual type of flat-bed view camera. The Swiss make a Synar, which is perhaps the best made, as well as the most expensive. The 5 × 7 Pico is slow in setting up and cumbersome in the field, but it is more definitive than a Deardorff and produces wonderful results. A disadvantage of the Synar is that you must have another half of a camera when you wish to adapt the 5 × 7 size to 4 × 5. I have the Pico fitted with an additional 4 × 5 back which has been especially adjusted to take the 4 × 5 Polaroid back at the exact same focal plane as the 5 × 7. This enables me to make tests with the Polaroid on 4 × 5 film without touching the focusing on the 5 × 7 image. Professional photographers will find this especially important in pre-judging elaborate set-ups.

There are other special cameras for special subjects. One of these is the Japanese Panon. This exposes film which is arranged in an arc opposite a moving lens and produces a 140-degree image, 2¼ × 4¼, with six pictures on a 120 roll. A 35mm model is also made. The photograph of the Tetons (pages 56-57) was made with the 120 Panon. Before the advent of this camera, except for the unwieldy panorama camera, commonly used for banquets, it was necessary to use a panorama tripod head when making pictures of especially wide horizontal areas. With this equipment, using great care, several continuous pictures could be made which were later joined together to produce a true panoramic view.

An unusual use of the Panon was made by George Silk in his brilliant color photographs on skiing. He took some of the photographs with the camera attached to the front of one of his skis. After fully exploiting the Panon for these special effects, Silk then decided that the strip camera used on race tracks to record the finish would produce even greater distortion in an interesting way. He then made the original pictures of the Olympic athletes with the strip camera. Two of these are shown on pages 130-131.

There are two extreme wide-angle cameras which contain built-in lenses. One is nicknamed the Syringe by its admirers, and the other the Fisheye. Yale Joel of *Life* has made something of a reputation with the Syringe. The center of the lens of this camera has a flywheel in front of it which must be rotated during the exposure. This is done so that the light passing through the extremely short lens is kept even over the entire film surface. The flywheel is activated by a bulb syringe, squeezed during the exposure. The extraordinary photograph of the new Time and Life Building shown on page 129 was made by Mr. Joel from the building itself by passing the camera out from the roof on a plank. The same photographer has also made use of the Syringe at parties and has transformed some comparatively dull subjects into really exciting pictures. The Nikon Fisheye is so called because the front of the camera looks like a huge fisheye. Ralph Morse employed this very-wide-angle camera to make the remarkable picture of the Metropolitan Opera House during a performance of *Don Giovanni* (page 132). Every part of the interior of the opera house is revealed in a 180-degree angle.

A final few words about cameras. I never, on any *important* assignment, use less than two different cameras and lenses. I sometimes use two different kinds of film, Kodachrome for high contrast, Ektachrome for muted effects. The reason for this is clear: to eliminate the danger of camera, lens, or film failure. With many subjects you can shoot with a 35mm and 50mm lens to obtain different effects. It is much wiser to use each lens on a different camera body and in that way be certain of your results. There are also times when a roll of film is ruined, and if the subject has been made on two cameras there is that much less chance of disappointment. This is especially important when the picture cannot be repeated or has been expensive to arrange—particularly to professionals who cannot afford technical failure.

LENSES

After twenty-five years in photography I must still honestly admit that I know almost nothing about lenses. I have never studied photo-optics, or taken a lens apart, or concerned myself with how many elements each type of lens has. My only concern in this field has been whether the lens is sharp, and whether it has been color-corrected. The analysis of lenses is too complex a field for the average working photographer; on the other hand, the quality of photography that various lenses produce is very much his concern. The primary advice about dealing with this entire question is to *test*. The photographer who buys a lens without testing its ability is making a serious mistake. The lens need not be examined on an optical bench by an expert; inexpensive charts are made which can be photographed indoors with the lens in question to test its resolving power. Also, making a photograph outdoors of a distant building will demonstrate the ability of the lens to produce sharp detail. Fine-grain film should be used in these tests; otherwise the grain pattern will interfere with maximum sharpness.

It is impossible to expect the highest-speed lenses to be as sharp as those designed for maximum sharpness without high speed. In the 35mm field, the demand by some photographers for higher-speed lenses has resulted

NOTES ON PLATES (pages 129-132)

129 TIME AND LIFE BUILDING.
By Yale Joel, with wide-angle "Syringe" camera set on a plank extended from the roof of the building.

130-31 OLYMPIC TRIALS, PALO ALTO, JUNE 1960.
By George Silk, with a strip camera.

132 METROPOLITAN OPERA HOUSE.
By Ralph Morse; made during a performance with a Nikon "Fisheye" camera.

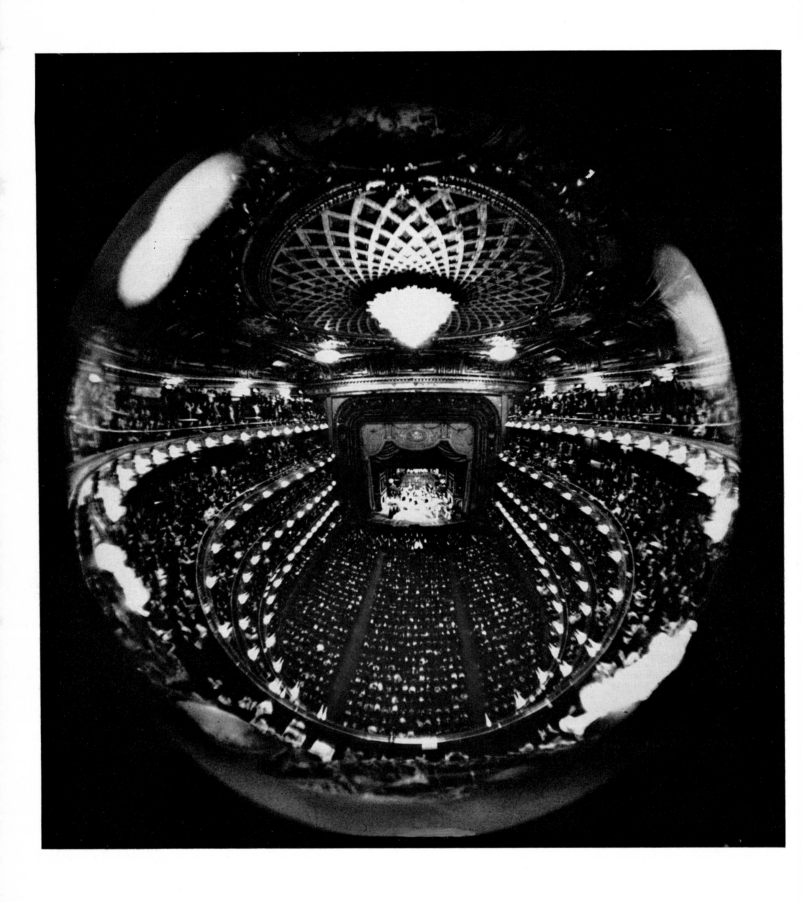

in new ones that are faster than F1. I have found that the 50mm F1.8 in the Canon group is a good combination of speed and sharpness. The Zeiss Sonnar 50mm F1.5 is again an excellent lens, and so is the Leitz Summicron of the same speed. One of the best lenses made today is the Nikon 58 mm F1.4 which combines high speed and sharpness. The photographs on pages 44 and 45 were both made at maximum aperture, F1.4. In the picture on page 44, taken at 1/30, advantage was made of the colorful and interesting low-key lighting used during the actual performance. The photograph of a Geisha lighting a patron's cigarette was taken at 1/8 second utilizing the actual light from the flame. Pictures such as these are only possible with high-speed lenses. Although 50mm is considered the normal focal length for the 35mm camera, many photographers find it their least-used lens. Nevertheless, it must be included in any well-balanced lens group. In addition to the 50mm, any standard outfit must include a wide-angle and a medium telephoto lens. If the outfit must be limited to three lenses I would recommend a 28mm and a 100mm as the additional ones.

With the 28mm lens the photographer can cope with most crowded interiors, produce dramatic perspective, and get semi-panoramic effects outdoors. The 105mm is an ideal focal length for head portraits and will allow the photographer to capture events without getting right on top of them. It is not, however, long enough for sports or wild-animal photography. My own outfit consists of 21mm, 28mm, 35mm, 58mm, 105mm, 200mm, and 350mm, and four Nikon F bodies. A recent development in lens design for still cameras has been the Nikon Zoom lens which adjusts from 85mm to 200mm or any point in between. It is a beautifully constructed lens, though a bit heavy for keeping permanently on one camera box. For some photographers it may be the perfect long-lens group all in one instrument.

In the $2\frac{1}{4} \times 2\frac{1}{4}$ field, the twin-lens reflexes offer no choice of lenses except when you buy the camera. I prefer the F2.8 Rolleiflex to the F3.5; it is useful to have the higher speed with color film. The single-lens reflex cameras offer a wide variety of lenses. Some photographers take advantage of the larger covering power of the old Zeiss 180mm and 300mm Sonnars, making use of them on both 35mm and $2\frac{1}{4} \times 2\frac{1}{4}$ bodies. These lenses are very sharp but also very heavy. Hasselblad offers

a good range of lenses that includes a 38mm wide-angle requiring its own separate body. A well-balanced outfit would be: 60mm Zeiss Disotar F5.6, 80mm Kodak Ektar F2.8, 135mm Kodak Ektar F3.5, and 250mm Zeiss Sonnar F4.

The $2\frac{1}{4} \times 3\frac{1}{4}$ Linhof may be purchased with three superb lenses: Zeiss Biogon 53mm F4.5, Zeiss Sonnar 100mm F2.8, Schneider Tele-Arton 240mm F5.5.

It is of course possible to add many more of any type to this outfit, since it is very simple to mount a lens on a Linhof metal lens board. The major problem, here and with 4×5 cameras, is whether to buy maximum-sharpness lenses of the Schneider Symmar type, whose maximum speed is F5.6, or to include Kodak Ektars or Zeiss Tessars, which are much faster in the normal focal lengths. I prefer the sharper double anastigmat type of the Schneider Symmar or Goerz Dagor. These lenses are extremely sharp and have great covering power as well. A lens of 15cm will cover a 5×7 area with perfect color to the corners without darkening. This enables the photographer to use camera movements such as the rising front with no anxiety about covering the film area.

A well-balanced lens outfit for a 4×5 camera, such as the Linhof or Deardorff, would be: 75mm Dagor, 150mm Symmar, 240mm Symmar. For a professional outfit, I would enlarge the group to include: 75mm Dagor, 100mm Dagor, 150mm Symmar, 210mm Symmar, and 400mm Tele-Magor.

I have all my large-camera lenses mounted in Linhof Boards, and use an adapter to fit them into the 5×7 Pico camera. This gives me a much greater variety without additional cost. My present outfit is a conglomeration of many years and is far from ideal, but the following is what I have. Exclusively for the Linhof (which will not cover the 5×7 film) I have 75mm Dagor F9, 100mm Dagor F8, 127mm Ektar F4.7. For both cameras I use 120mm Aristostigmat 6.3, 150mm Symmar F5.6, 180mm Symmar F6.8, 210mm Symmar F5.6, 240mm Symmar F6.8, 400mm Tele-Magor F5.6. This would seem to be a lot of lenses, but each one of them is well used. Lenses should be fitted with special shutters permitting built-in synchronization with both flash and strobe.

The 8×10 view camera used in the studio should have a 10-, 12-, and 14-inch double anastigmat lens group, and if it is to be used for architecture and interiors an 8-inch or shorter lens should also be included.

The two most popular meters for gauging exposure are the Weston and Norwood. The Weston measures light reflected from the object, whereas the Norwood measures the light itself. Both have their advantages and advocates, and when used properly both will produce satisfactory results. The most important thing is to know what you are photographing. You cannot point a Weston meter at a subject which includes bright sky and a person in partial shade twenty feet away and obtain a satisfactory reading. The reading in this case will be for the sky, but is it the sky you wish to photograph? That is the problem in a nutshell. Decide which is the most important object or area in your picture and measure the light of that object or area with your meter. If you are using a Norwood meter, then you must also take into account the darkness or lightness of your subject, because this makes a difference too. Dark subjects need a longer exposure than light ones.

Another simple principle in color photography is that the shadow area of a subject usually looks much more attractive as a dark mass than a bright portion looks when it is over-exposed. The meter assists us in discovering whether or not one of the areas must be sacrificed without additional lighting, since color film has a very shallow range in obtaining both dark and light. Making exposure notes at the time of photographing is a good way to improve color techniques, and light readings on several parts of the subject should be noted as well.

Bracketing is one positive way of assuring perfect exposure. This technique consists of determining correct exposure with the meter, then, after taking the photograph, taking two additional exposures, one with the lens open one stop more than the meter indicates, and one with it set at one stop less. This gives the photographer a hundred-per-cent margin of exposure error either way. Some photographers, especially professionals who must produce a perfect exposure, often give an additional pair of exposures, halving the stops. To F4, 5.6, and 8 they add one between F4 and 5.6, and one between F5.6 and 8. Some photographers add another stop in either direction rather than halving the stops, in order to get greater width on the exposure range. This is a matter of personal preference and should depend on the subject itself. I have found that if the subject is very contrasty it pays to try exposures for both ends of an extreme scale because it is not always apparent which will be more desirable. In ordinary subjects a half-stop either way from normal is the best method by which you can obtain perfect density.

In addition to the two meters mentioned, several others have their supporters. The General Electric meter is one of these. Both the German and the Japanese have pioneered in smaller meters and have made some which can be fitted on top of the camera. These are accurate enough, and may be used in the same way as the larger ones. Some cameras today have built-in meters that actually control the exposure. I recently checked one of these and found that the meter often reacted to the strong light from the sky and underexposed the rest of the picture. It will be some time before these automatic cameras are completely satisfactory, except to the amateur looking for short cuts.

The reader should also be cautioned about reciprocity. This simply means that very long or very short exposures on color film reduce the speed of the emulsion and perhaps change its color as well. Sheet color film is especially subject to these changes, and the instruction sheet in the box of film indicates such loss and recommends corrective filters where necessary.

In addition to exposure meters there are meters that measure color temperature. I have still to be convinced of their accuracy and usefulness. I have bought and discarded several of them and find that experience is more help than anything else. There are also exposure meters for flash and strobe light which are both accurate and expensive. Many professionals use the Polaroid camera to check such exposures and eliminate the need for either meters or wide bracketing. However, as was mentioned once before, a neutral-density filter of the correct strength should be utilized to make the speed of the Polaroid film equal the color film. See page 154 for chart on which N.D. is required for various films.

Most photographers do not develop their own color film but send it to a laboratory. An excellent guide for those who wish to do their own color developing is given in Andreas Feininger's excellent textbook, *Successful Color Photography* (New York: Prentice-Hall, 1955). Laboratories are not foolproof, and they have in fact often unwittingly altered a color film and occasionally ruined it altogether. The biggest problem is the lack of constancy in the manufacture of color film. Kodachrome has been constant, but every other emulsion has its own individual characteristics of color and speed. These characteristics are indicated in the instruction sheet included in color-film packages, but they are not always entirely accurate. Herbert Orth, the brilliant technician who heads the *Life* color laboratory, tests for both color and speed every new emulsion of color film bought by the magazine. This service may also be obtained from commercial color laboratories.

A good deal of the cut film manufactured today requires a delicate compensating filter to provide color balance. It seems that it is almost impossible to manufacture the film without some variance. Occasionally a batch comes through that requires no filter. The laboratory may also alter the development of the color film slightly in order to correct for underexposure or overexposure. This was normal procedure with Ektachrome 1 at the *Life* lab but it is not entirely possible with Ektachrome 3. Herbert Orth and I have worked out a technique known as the "split holder." By giving the two films in a cut-film holder exactly the same exposure and developing only one film, the second one may be adjusted in development after the first has been inspected. This technique may also be used with roll film shooting a few exposures on the beginning of the roll, cutting these exposures off (usually ruining one frame), and developing them for inspection before the remainder of the film is processed.

COLOR FILMS

Choice of film must often depend upon camera size, and sometimes upon the type of subject material. Kodachrome has long been the most popular color film with both amateurs and professionals who use a 35mm camera. A new Kodachrome emulsion, Kodachrome II, has just been developed which increases the speed of this film from ASA 10 to 25, with a considerable decrease in contrast. The latter will be a blow to amateurs who have always appreciated the over-brilliance of this film, but the new emulsion gives results that are much closer to reality, and the higher speed is, of course, a benefit to all. A new, faster Ektachrome is another Eastman development with a speed of ASA160 for the daylight emulsion. The film is available in both 35mm and 120. The regular 35mm Ektachrome remains at ASA25 or 32, depending upon development, although it is rated at 50 by the manufacturer. Ansco manufactures a 35mm film called Anscochrome with an ASA of 32, as well as high-speed emulsion.

The new Eastman High Speed Ektachrome mentioned above is now in constant use by *Life* photographers who must be able to produce color photographs under any light conditions. In the summer of 1961 I made extensive use of this film when I photographed "Japan After Dark" (pages 44 and 45). Grain in these pictures does not distract from the mood of the story which is principally in low key. The photograph of the Geisha hostess lighting a patron's cigarette (page 45) was made by the light from the cigarette lighter, plus an imperceptible touch of soft bounce light to keep the scene from being almost completely black. "Follies, Nichigeki Theatre"

(page 44) was made during an actual performance without additional lighting. This story would have been impossible to do, and have it appear realistic, without High Speed Ektachrome. The speed of the incandescent (tungsten) Ektachrome I used was ASA 100.

By examining several emulsion tests on a variety of colors in the laboratory the photographer can choose either Ektachrome or Ansco, depending on which colors are most important to his subject. I have, at times, used two different emulsions on one subject so that I can choose the better one after development. The larger cameras such as 2¼ × 2¼ and 2¼ × 3¼ can use the faster films without too much grain problem, but these emulsions are not available for the large camera requiring sheet film.

Negative color such as Kodacolor has become very popular, especially with photographers who wish to make their own color prints. One of the disadvantages of this process, however, is the difficulty of rendering pure color, but its use is growing steadily with amateurs.

Kodachrome F (for flash bulbs) and Kodachrome A (for 3200 incandescent lighting) can be used outdoors with the proper correcting filters. See chart, page 154.

FILTERS

The use of filters has been dealt with in previous chapters. Nevertheless, a recapitulation of some of the points already made may serve to crystallize in the reader's mind the variety and color qualities of the types available. Eastman Kodak makes the Skylight filter, which I use most of the time in outdoor photography. Its function is to lessen the effect of the blue light from the sky, especially when no direct sunlight is illuminating the subject. This filter requires no increase in exposure. Contrary to popular belief, the Skylight filter is not the same as the U.V. (ultraviolet) filter made by other manufacturers. The U.V. is usually a light tan, in contrast to the pink quality of the Skylight.

A group of important filters manufactured by Harrison and Harrison in Hollywood are light-correction filters which were designed for balancing color film to different Kelvin lighting but are also useful in color control outdoors, as has already been explained. The C series, coral in color, acts as a warmer in daylight, adding a slight umber tone to the over-all scene. The lightest of this series, C⅛, is extremely useful to remove excess blue light on a rainy day. The C¼ gives a stronger effect. The B series, which are bluish-green in color, will produce a cooler picture. These filters come in ⅛, ¼, ½, 1, and 2 strengths. The chart on page 153 indicates the increased exposure necessary for all the B and C series.

Eastman Kodak makes two series of filters similar to the Harrison B and C, the 81 and 82 series. The 81 warms and the 82 cools. The chart on page 153 indicates the relative values between the Kodak 81 and 82 and the Harrison series.

Kodak also makes the Color Compensating series known as CC. These come in six types: yellow, magenta (pink), cyan (blue-green), red, green, and blue. They are available in six strengths: 05, 10, 20, 30, 40, and 50. The chart on page 153 indicates the necessary increase in exposure for these filters. I seldom use a more powerful one than CC 20. Three different examples of the use of these filters have been reproduced in this book: the blue one in the waterfall picture (page 73), the green one in the oil-palms picture (page 74), and the yellow one in the photograph of the women pounding grain (page 75).

Another useful filter, the Wratten K1, often used to emphasize cloud effects in black-and-white photography, can be used with color film, too, for special effects. The photograph of the becalmed boats (page 43) and the girl on the bridge (page 47) were both made with the K1 filter. It requires a ¼ to ½ stop increase in exposure.

The polarizer filter will darken a sky, especially near the horizon, and will bring out distant detail by eliminating or lessening reflections. The required increase of exposure is four times more than the meter indicates.

Finally, there are the diffuser filters or diffusing disks. These cut down the sharpness of the lens. The Harrison series is called Fog Filters and is made in 5 strengths, 1 to 5. I use only the 3 and 5. Kodak makes diffusion disks which can be used for the same purpose. All require a slight increase in exposure.

SPECIAL PROBLEMS   *Aerial Photography*

The best cameras for this work, except for the ponderous professional ones, are the 35mm and 2¼ × 2¼ size models. A great many of my 35mm Kodachromes have been enlarged satisfactorily for full-page and double-page reproductions in *Life*. The fine grain of Kodachrome makes this film an excellent choice for the detail desirable in aerial views. Furthermore, the high contrast of Kodachrome helps in overcoming haze. The use of a Skylight filter is recommended at all times. The most satisfactory choice of lens for aerial photography is the 50mm or 85mm, either of which help in making pictures without the intrusion of the plane fuselage or wing.

Aerial photographers find that the lower the airplane the higher the shutter speed necessary to achieve a sharp picture. Generally speaking, a shutter speed of less than 1/250 second is inadvisable except at high altitudes. It is not easy to obtain good results through glass or plastic windows, even when they have been specially washed and are not too scratched. The clearer the day, the clearer the picture.

I prefer single-lens reflex cameras for aerial photography because with them you can be sure you are not getting part of the window edge or strut into the picture. With a rangefinder camera the small distance between the finder on top of the camera and the taking lens is often just great enough to result in a picture that is partly cut into by the window. The 2¼ × 2¼ single-lens reflex, as well as the twin-lens Rolleiflex, are both excellent types for aerial photography.

If you can charter a plane, the best ones are small planes such as Cubs and Cessnas. Both types permit removal of a door, or fastening the side window out of the way. Never lean on a door, and, because of vibration, never rest your camera on any part of the plane.

Helicopters are excellent to photograph from, but the pilot should not be asked to hover too long, for the vibration that usually sets in can blur your pictures.

A plan in the form of a drawing of the approach to the subject should be made before going up; furthermore, some kind of hand signals should be agreed upon between you and the pilot. Do not ask the pilot to break any laws about minimum altitude, no matter how tempting this may be. Let him fly his own plane. Sometimes a pilot can be too eager to help. Terence Spencer, who lives in South Africa and free-lances for *Life*, is an ex-RAF pilot who owns his own plane. He took me up over Johannesburg in 1959 to make some pictures of Sophiatown. His idea of ideal aerial photographic technique is to make an almost direct approach to the target, turn the plane so that your side is just opposite this target, and then slow the plane almost to a stall so you have as long as possible to take a sharp picture. He did this about six times, each time coming a little closer to a real stall at about three hundred feet. I appreciated his zeal, but would have been quite happy with less!

Medical Photography

This is an even more specialized field. Many physicians, especially surgeons, make their own medical records for lectures and publication. Most of them use the single-lens reflex 35mm camera, which offers them equal opportunities in general photography as well. I have suggested to some surgeons a special mount right over the operating table with a remote cable release which permits them to keep the camera out of the way while an operation is in progress. The correct filter may be determined by testing the balance of the operating lights to the color film.

Some of the problems of medical photography pertain to other fields in which extreme close-ups are required. Most 35mm and 2¼ × 2¼ cameras can be fitted with supplementary lenses or extension tubes and bellows to permit close-up work. A special 35mm lens made by Kilfit in Germany has its own built-in extension barrel which permits extreme close-ups. Markings on the barrel also indicate magnification increase as well as exposure increase when the lens extends beyond its own focal length from the film plane. Kodak puts out a table for increase in exposures due to bellows extension. For photographing small objects, an even light is usually a prerequisite. Many doctors use a small round strobe-light unit made to fit completely around the lens to give even illumination.

Under-Water Photography

In this field Peter Stackpole has probably done as much as or more than anyone else. He manufactures excellent plastic bodies, available at better photographic stores, to house both 35mm and 2¼ × 2¼ cameras for use under water.

The most important aspect of under-water photography is knowing the limitations of daylight in deep or murky water. A Skylight filter can be used to cut down the blue effect unless this effect is particularly desirable, and in some instances it might be. Electronic or ordinary flash may also be used in special cases, as well as waterproof tungsten lights to illuminate subjects in deep water. Taking pictures through the windows of an aquarium or pool is comparatively simple, provided these are well lit. The exposure meter will indicate the right setting, but it must be remembered that the reading will register the highlights of the water, not facial or body detail. If this is important, exposures should be increased by one stop after taking the general reading. In other words, if the meter indicates a setting of 1/50 at F5.6, you should shoot at F4.

Unless you are using artificial light under water it is advisable to make your pictures at noon when maximum sunlight is pouring straight down. This is particularly necessary when photographing under-water scenes from a glass-bottom boat. Only in the shallowest water and with the lightest-colored rock backgrounds are such pictures likely to produce results that are at all worth while. A more than usual element of luck is involved here because finding the most interestingly colored fish in sufficiently shallow water and with adequate natural light is not a common occurrence. Furthermore, the boat itself casts a shadow, and shooting through glass windows more often than not requires a flash or artificial under-water light to get good, clear results.

Heat

Heat is the great enemy of color film. Do not leave your camera in the sun. It is just the same as if you were to place the film in a lighted oven. A closed car and, worse still, the trunk of a car are almost as bad as an oven if the day is really hot. Color film will not survive this kind of treatment. It is good policy not to leave the roll in the camera too long, especially in hot, humid places such as the seashore or in semi-tropical climates.

Color film is marked with an expiration date. Do not use it after that date, particularly if it has not been stored in a cool place. Kodachrome is the most stable film made, but it will suffer if mistreated. Some photographers keep their color film in a refrigerator. In very hot climates this is a good idea, but it must be remembered that condensation will take place on the film after it comes into warmer air. It is absolutely essential, therefore, to wait at least four hours to allow the film to return to normal temperature before using it in the camera.

I was once faced with the problem of keeping color film cool while taking pictures in Egypt during the summer. The temperature was 110 or more. The fresh film was sent from Cairo to Luxor in the refrigerator of the overnight train. When it arrived I loaded the film into 4 × 5 holders. These were put into a small metal clothes trunk which in turn was placed in a large wooden crate. The crate was then covered with a half-dozen burlap bags which were thoroughly soaked just before our party left for the trip. A man carrying a water bag continued to soak the burlap every once in a while so that evaporation of the water would keep the case cool. The exposed film was unloaded each day, packed between dried black papers, and sent to Cairo on the return train to be airexpressed to New York. Under these conditions, the sooner the film is developed the better. The humidity from the water was a hazard, but the tin inner case kept most of it out. Silica gel, a chemical that absorbs humidity, would have been useful to combat this.

Perhaps the most important comment to be made about equipment is that it must be a completely personal choice. Every photographer has different hands and different reactions to the position of controls. He must find the camera that he can handle best and that is most suited to the kind of photography he wants to do. Actually the camera, lens, meter, tripod, film, and other equipment are the least important aspects of photography. Great photographs have been made with the least expensive instruments, and it is equally true that no amount of expensive equipment alone, will ever produce a great photograph. It is the eye, the mind, and the heart that make great photographs.

◼ 8

AN APPRECIATION

There are still no clear standards by which to judge photography. Although the medium is well over a century old, comparatively little critical appraisal has been devoted to it. Photography critics similar to those writing about music, drama, literature, film, and art are practically nonexistent, and the standards of excellence are consequently none too well defined. My standards, for whatever they are worth, are as follows:

1. A photograph must *look* like a photograph; if it doesn't, why use a camera?

2. A photograph should be well made technically, include deliberate photographic deviation when the subject demands it, and be well designed aesthetically.

3. A picture should express a point of view, a sentiment, or thought.

4. Additional credit should be given a photographer for originality.

The question of whether photography is or can be an art has plagued many people, both in and out of photography. In my opinion, some photography is art although it is executed with a mechanical object, the camera. The fact that all paintings have been produced laboriously by hand does not make all of them works of art. The actual physical recording of the photographic image is the least vital aspect of photography. No one seriously claims that the billions of snapshots made today are works of art, and some say none are. Photographs that transcend the medium of their making by infusing the subject with values, that inspire the viewer with new ideas and new dimensions, and that give the audience a richer world to look at and understand surely must be considered art.

There are not many photographers who are great artists for the same reason that there aren't many great artists in other creative fields either. In these concluding pages I have assembled a few pictures by photographers whom I consider to be among the best in their respective fields today. These men have consistently produced photographs which are uniquely their own and whose style is readily recognizable. Not all of them are color photographers exclusively. In fact, several are known only for their black-and-white pictures.

Although Henri Cartier-Bresson occasionally works in color, he is properly famous for his remarkable black-and-white pictures of people made with the 35mm camera, (see page 142). His photographs, always made in the most unobtrusive way possible, contain a combination of personal intellectual appreciation of the social mores of our time plus a superb sense of pictorial composition. None of his pictures even suggests posing or direction, and the composition seems just to have happened instead of being highly sought for. This school of photography has grown enormously in the last few years, and several of Cartier-Bresson's major followers, such as Bruce Davison, Elliott Erwitt, and Inge Morath, are achieving their own positions.

Another photographer of this type, Cornell Capa, is distinguished for his acute social sense as were his distinguished colleagues and my good friends David (Chim) Seymour and Robert Capa, Cornell's brother (see page 147). Alfred Eisenstadt, Leonard McCombe, and Carl Mydans are other photographers who have employed the 35mm camera to make an extraordinary record of our time.

There are many fine craftsmen, especially among the magazine photographers who have used as great a variety of equipment as the variety of their subject material demanded. Emil Schulthess, the Swiss photographer, has published three fine books on the United States, Antarctica, and Africa, which reveal him as one of our contemporary masters. No subject has been too difficult, too small, or too distant to escape his lens (see page 144). Lately he has specialized in photographing the sun and moon. He combines technical virtuosity with an acute visual sense of the patterns and beauties of nature. Andreas Feininger, Tom Hollyman, Fritz Goro, Dmitri Kessel, and John Lewis Stage are among those who share this gift.

Irving Penn is a tireless experimenter in color photography, known for a variety of work published in *Vogue* as well as for his commercial illustrations and for the book on his work published in 1960. His photographs of baseball and bullfighting are among the first to utilize large grain and blur to make color photography more expressive. His experiments in color distortion in the deBeers diamond advertisements are among the most

revolutionary attempted in the commercial field. His 1953 shot of three different wines being poured (page 146), and one of champagne, have inspired endless copies. His black-and-white fashion and portrait photographs are equally exciting. Erwin Blumenfeld, too, has made many brilliant color experiments, especially with the human figure. Gordon Parks included in his portfolio on American poetry a photograph of Brooklyn Bridge which is one of his best (page 145). He has utilized color distortion and multiple exposure to add poetic dimension to his work. Parks, who is equally gifted as a musician and composer, also produced one of the most difficult picture stories ever published in *Life*, on a Harlem street gang.

Richard Avedon, one of the first photographers to work with blur and with the whitened face, also produces highly personal photographs in both portraiture and the theater. Arnold Newman's portraits are unmistakably his. The group of photographs he produced for *Holiday* on the American Indian represent a masterpiece of historical portraiture, as exciting as the paintings of George Catlin.

Alfred Steiglitz was the poet-photographer prototype. He used cloud formations as the theme for his series of pictures called "Equivalents," one of the first attempts to abstract patterns of nature. Edward Weston later did the same thing with eroded rocks, twisted roots, bits of vegetables, seaweed, and other interestingly shaped objects that came to his eye. He did these in superb and magnificent glowing 8 × 10 black-and-white contact prints of unbelievable quality. His book, *My Camera on Point Lobos* (Boston: Houghton, Mifflin, 1950) is an extraordinary photographic tour de force. "Green Pepper" (page 141) I am extremely proud to have in my own collection. Another Californian, Ansel Adams, is also devoting himself to landscape photography of remarkable quality. Two more photographers, both of whom teach at the Institute of Design in Chicago, Aaron Siskind and Tom Callahan, have brilliantly carried this tradition to the minutiae of cities.

Then there is Ernest Haas, the poet-photographer, to whom subject material is completely secondary to his own expression. His portfolio on bullfighting utilized blur as no one ever has. An exciting experiment of this type with sailboats is reproduced on page 143. Haas's work in Venice and New York captured the reflections of each of these cities and recreated their multiple dimensions. He is happy to photograph anything and mold it with his own ideas and technique to create something totally new. There are many other men who should be mentioned in an appreciation, both in the fields of black-

and-white and color photography. Some have already been noted in previous chapters. There is, of course, Edward Steichen, who has had as much and perhaps more general influence on portraiture than anyone. In black-and-white, the Englishman Bill Brandt is an outstanding poet-photographer. His book, *Literary Britain* (New York: British Book Centre, 1951), is a masterpiece, and his new book on nudes is a most original treatment. Brassai, like Brandt, works primarily in black-and-white, and has recorded the life of his city, Paris, with great sensitivity. In sports both Mark Kaufmann and Hy Peskin have utilized color for heightened impression; Kaufmann particularly innovated with extreme telephoto lenses, and Peskin with his superb sense of action. Gjon Mili, a long-ago student of Dr. Harold Edgerton of the Massachusetts Institute of Technology, who invented stroboscopic lighting, took this scientific tool and introduced it into everyday photography through the artistry of his technique. Howard Sochurek has immersed himself in the jet-plane age and created new pictorial images which are in key with his subject. Ralph Morse has done the same not only with astronautics but with everyday journalistic photography.

The young photographer William Klein should also be mentioned here, although he works primarily in black-and-white. His photographic books on New York (an example from which is shown on page 148) and Rome demonstrate the brilliant and deliberate use of very coarse grain, underexposure with heavy blanks and overexposure with pure white areas, blurred action, fuzzy focus, and sometimes unbalanced compositions. All these devices, which might be termed anti-photographic, are used to remove the onus of technical perfection desired by some photographers. If there is such a thing as beatnik photography, then I would say Klein is the leader.

Dennis Stock also produced a fine book—on jazz—using a similar approach.

In conclusion, I would like to pay special tribute to Margaret Bourke-White, the Richard Harding Davis prototype of photo-journalism, who did more than anyone else to set the pace for modern magazine photography.

NOTES ON PLATES (pages 141-148)

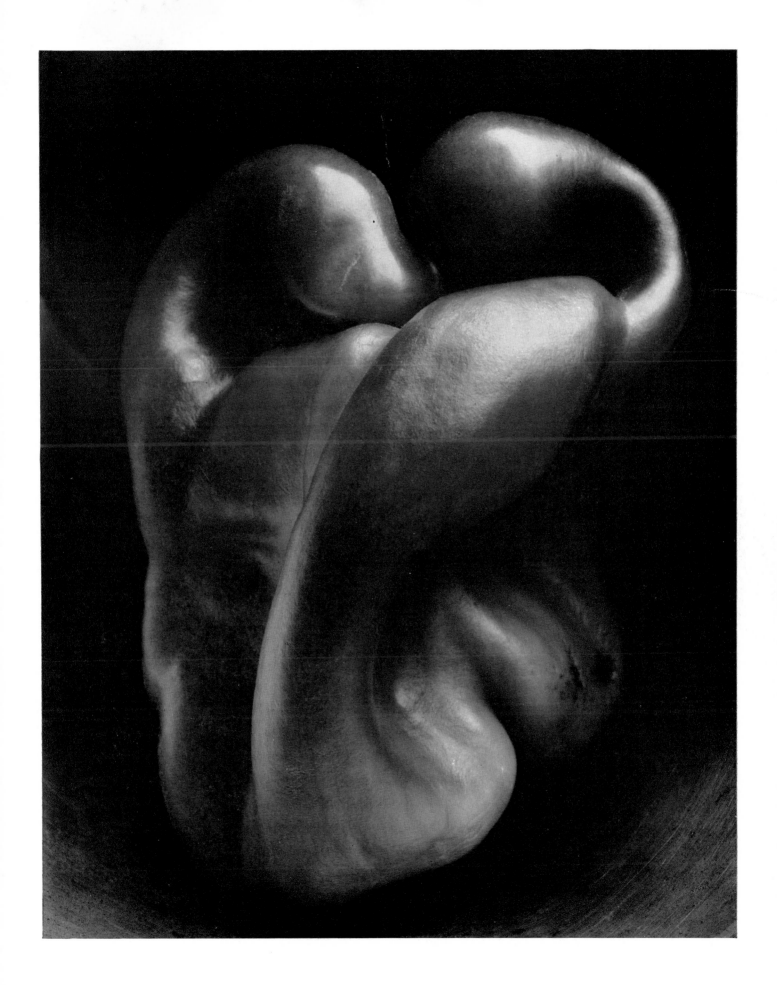

DO'S AND DON'T'S

The following notes summarize a few of the points made in the foregoing chapters. They are printed here as a check list of special things to consider doing or avoid when you set out to take color photographs.

Don't overload your picture with color just because you have paid for color film. A lot of color does not necessarily make a good color picture. Do not look for obvious color; look for the subtle.

Keep your subjects simple. The introduction of too many distracting elements will ruin a picture.

In portrait work, don't use complicated backgrounds; these will compete with the subject unless they are related to it intrinsically. Consider using out-of-focus backgrounds.

Landscapes are dull when there is too much unused space, such as an unimportant foreground or sky. Move in on what you are taking instead of dissipating the effect with a lot of nothing. Look for unusual sky and sea effects.

Consider the use of filters to correct color and to create special effects.

Don't always wait for sun to take landscapes. Nature provides the most help in adding strange light or a great stormy sky or a ray of sunlight breaking through heavy clouds. Learn to look for pictures when the weather is supposedly "all wrong" for photography, as in heavy rainfall. (I carry a sawed-off umbrella in my tripod case, ready for such occasions.) Take some pictures at dawn and at twilight.

Don't make technically difficult photographs without taking careful notes of everything you do. This way you can learn from your mistakes. Keep a small notebook in your camera case and force yourself to use it.

Don't succumb to the camera fever of trading in your equipment every time you see someone else with another, newer camera. It is not the camera that counts as much as it is the eye, heart, and brain of the photographer. Stick to one good camera until you have mastered it.

Make the camera a part of your fingers. Learn to operate it without worrying whether you are doing the right thing, such as setting the right focus and exposure. If you are involved in mechanics you will have nothing inspirational to give to the subject.

Buy the best outfit you can afford. You cannot save money by buying cheap equipment, because you will get nothing for it when you trade it in. It is more economical to start with the best.

Read art books and go to your local art museum and study the compositions of both classic and modern artists. Analyze their paintings and discover why they have divided their canvas into thirds or fourths for earth and sky, where the head is placed on a bust portrait and full-length. Photographers have much to learn from great artists about the problems of composition and color.

Read the camera magazines; *U.S. Camera*, *Popular Photography*, and *Modern Photography* are all excellent and give ideas and technical information to their readers.

Don't be bound by anyone's rules or dogmatic approach, least of all mine. Make up your own mind and try anything you like. But develop an eye for the good result so that even if you make it accidentally you can recognize a good picture instead of throwing it away.

If you are young and are thinking of taking up photography as a profession, consider going to a good school. There are several in the United States that give solid training in this highly skilled and extremely competitive field. I prefer the schools where painting is taught as well as photography because I feel that design is one of the most important elements in photography.

VIRGINIA MAYO See page 116

LIGHTING DIAGRAMS

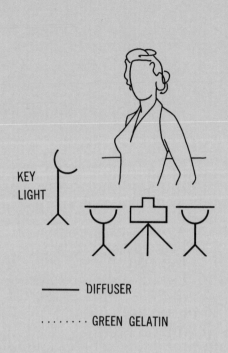

KEY
LIGHT

KEY
LIGHT

————— DIFFUSER

·········· GREEN GELATIN

KEY
LIGHT

MONTREAL BALL   See page 91

$\frac{1}{50}$ — F22
DAYLIGHT — EKTACHROME
*ASCOR STROBE UNITS

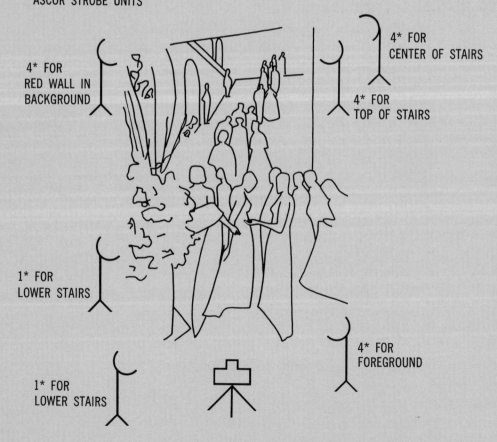

4* FOR
RED WALL IN
BACKGROUND

4* FOR
CENTER OF STAIRS

4* FOR
TOP OF STAIRS

1* FOR
LOWER STAIRS

4* FOR
FOREGROUND

1* FOR
LOWER STAIRS

PYRAMIDS See page 87

1 SEC — F22
½ SEC — F32
1 SEC — F32

F.C.
TABLE — 50
GARDEN — 100

4 — G.E. #50
BLUE FLASH — EKTACHROME

FOR PEOPLE
AT TABLE

FOR TREE AND
CHAMPAGNE BOTTLE

LIGHTS NEAR CAMERA
DOUBLE DIFFUSED —
7 FEET FROM TABLE

SET-UP FOR SCULPTURE

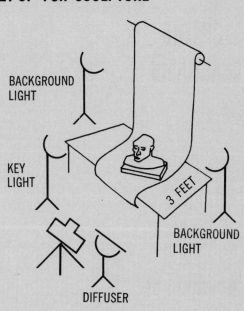

BACKGROUND
LIGHT

KEY
LIGHT

3 FEET

BACKGROUND
LIGHT

DIFFUSER

UNIVERSITY OF MEXICO MEDICAL LECTURE See page 90

1/50 — F5.6
DAYLIGHT KODACHROME

LIGHTS TRIPPED BY
PHOTO ELECTRIC CELLS

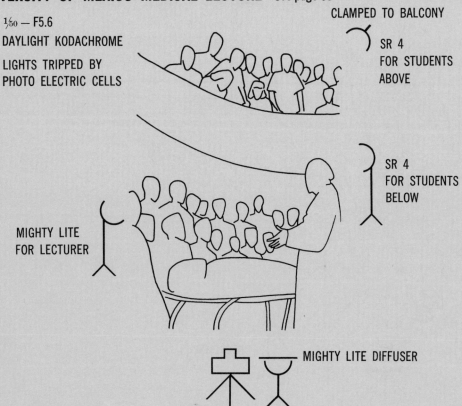

CLAMPED TO BALCONY

SR 4
FOR STUDENTS
ABOVE

SR 4
FOR STUDENTS
BELOW

MIGHTY LITE
FOR LECTURER

MIGHTY LITE DIFFUSER

APPROXIMATE CONVERSION AND COMPARISON
OF VARIOUS SPEED RATING TABLES

A.S.A.*	Weston	General Electric	Din	A.S.A.*	Weston	General Electric	Din
1.0	0.7	1	1/10	32	24	40	16/10
1.2	1.0	1.5	2/10	40	32	48	17/10
1.6	1.2	2	3/10	50	40	64	18/10
2.0	1.5	2.5	4/10	64	50	80	19/10
2.5	2.0	3	5/10	80	64	100	20/10
3	2.5	4	6/10	100	80	125	21/10
4	3	4.5	7/10	125	100	150	22/10
5	4	6	8/10	160	125	200	23/10
6	5	8	9/10	200	160	250	24/10
8	6	10	10/10	250	200	300	25/10
10	8	12	11/10	320	250	400	26/10
12	10	16	12/10	400	320	500	27/10
16	12	20	13/10	500	400	600	28/10
20	16	24	14/10	650	500	800	29/10
25	20	32	15/10	800	650	900	30/10
*American Standards Association film numbers				1000	800	1000	31/10

FILTERS

Color Compensating Filters

Yellow	EXPOSURE INCREASE	Magenta	EXPOSURE INCREASE	Cyan	EXPOSURE INCREASE
CC 05 Y	0	CC 05 M		CC 05 C	
CC 10 Y		CC 10 M	⅓ stop	CC 10 C	⅓ stop
CC 20 Y	⅓ stop	CC 20 M		CC 20 C	

Red		Green		Blue	
CC 05 R		CC 05 G		CC 05 B	
CC 10 R	⅓ stop	CC 10 G	⅓ stop	CC 10 B	⅓ stop
CC 20 R		CC 20 G		CC 20 B	

Light Balancing Filters

Bluish		EXPOSURE INCREASE	Yellowish		EXPOSURE INCREASE
Kodak	Harrison		Kodak	Harrison	
82	B ⅛		81		
82A	B ¼	⅓ stop	81A	C ⅛	
82B	B ½	⅔ stop	81B	C ¼	⅓ stop
			81C	C ½	
			81D		⅔ stop

To convert A Kodachrome to Daylight use No. 85 Filter.   **To convert B Ektachrome to Daylight use No. 85B Filter.**

To convert F Kodachrome or Ektachrome to Daylight use No. 85C Filter.

FLASH, FILTER, AND EXPOSURE DATA FOR COLOR FILMS

		KODACHROME A 35 MM	KODACHROME DAY 35 MM
	Daylight	ASA 10 85 filter	ASA 10
	Polaroid exposure guide with strobe		1.30 neutral density or 4⅓ stops
FLOOD	3200° K	ASA 12 82 filter	Not recommended
	3400° K	ASA 16	Not recommended
FLASH—See note A	Flash #5 1/25 sec. 22 50	Guide #55 90 81B filter 135	Guide #40 65 80C filter 85
	Flash #5B 1/25 sec. 22B 50B	Not recommended	Guide #40 65 85
STROBE—See note B	Stroboflash 1 2 3-4	Not recommended	Guide #28 45 56
	Ascor 602-610 1 lamp 4 lamps	Not recommended	Guide #125 250
	Multistrobe 1000 W	Not recommended	Guide #70
	Mightylite Mightylite de luxe	Not recommended	Guide #23 32

NOTE A: All the flash tests were made at 1/25th of a second using a satin reflector. These guide numbers may vary from ½ to 1 stop with various types of polished reflectors. At speeds other than 1/25th of a second the following adjustments are necessary: decrease the guide number 10 per cent for 1/50th of a second; 22 per cent for 1/100th; 40 per cent for 1/200th.

KODACHROME 11 DAY 35 MM	ANSCOCHROME DAY 35 MM, 120 AND SHEET FILM	ANSCOCHROME TUNGSTEN SHEET FILM	HIGH-SPEED EKTACHROME B E-2 35 MM AND 120	HIGH-SPEED EKTACHROME DAY E-2 35 MM AND 120	EKTACHROME DAY E-3 120 AND SHEET FILM	EKTACHROME B E-3 SHEET FILM
ASA 25	ASA 25	ASA 12 / 85B filter	ASA 64 / 85B filter	ASA 160	ASA 32	ASA 25 / 85B filter
.90 neutral density or 3 stops	.90 neutral density or 3 stops			.10 neutral density or 1/3 stop	.90 neutral density or 3 stops	
Not recommended	Not recommended	ASA 25	ASA 100	ASA 25 / 80+	Not recommended	ASA 32 / 1/2 sec. or faster
Not recommended	Not recommended	ASA 20 / 81A filter	ASA 80 / 81A filter	ASA 32 / 80B+	Not recommended	ASA 25 / 81A filter / 1/2 sec. or faster
Guide #80 / 80C filter 120 / 170	Guide #80 / 80C filter 120 / 170	Guide #55 / 81C filter 90 / 135	Guide #170 / 81C filter 280 / 400	Guide #160 / 80C filter 240 / 340	Guide #80 / 80C filter 120 / 170	Guide #130 / 81C filter 200 / 300
Guide #80 / 120 / 170	Guide #80 / 120 / 170	Not recommended	Not recommended	Guide #160 / 82 filter 240 / 340	Guide #80 / 82 filter 120 / 170	Not recommended
Guide #44 / 75 / 90	Guide #44 / 75 / 90	Not recommended	Guide #44 / 85B filter 75 / 90	Guide #88 / 150 / 180	Guide #40 / 62 / 80	Not recommended
Guide #210 / 420	Guide #210 / 420	Not recommended	Guide #210 / 85B filter 420	Guide #420 / 840	Guide #170 / 340	Not recommended
Guide #110	Guide #110	Not recommended	Guide #110 / 85B filter	Guide #220	Guide #95	Not recommended
Guide #35 / 50	Guide #35 / 50	Not recommended	Guide #35 / 85B filter 50	Guide #70 / 100	Guide #28 / 46	Not recommended

NOTE B: Filter required. Under normal conditions, the manufacturer's filter recommendation in the film package may be used.

FILM AND COLOR TEMPERATURE CHART

This chart shows relationship of film properties to color temperature of common light sources. It is to be used as a guide in selecting filters, such as whether to use a warming yellow or cooling blue filter, and does not specify exactly which gradation of filter will give the best results.

How to use the chart

If film is located on a line or position higher than a listed light source, rendition will be too yellowish or reddish without a filter. To remedy this, use a bluish or cooling filter.

If film is located on a line or position lower than a listed light source, rendition will be too blue without a filter. To remedy this, use a yellowish or warming filter.

Brackets (}) indicate where film and light source match and no filter is needed.

LIGHT SOURCE	COLOR TEMPERATURE	FILM
Blue Skylight	12,000–27,000 K	
Hazy, smoky sky	7500–8400 K	
Overcast	6800 K	
Electronic Flash[1]	5500–6800 K	
Sunlight	5000–6000 K	All daylight-type color films.
Blue-tinted flashlamps	6000 K	
Warm late-afternoon and early-morning sunlight	4300–4800 K	
Clear (white) foil-filled flashlamps	3800 K	Type F or flash-type color films.
Photoflood lamps Nos. 1, 2, and 4	3400 K	Type A or tungsten-type (3400 K) color films.
Gas-filled flashlamps, SM and SF[2]	3300 K	
3200 K flood, spot, and projection-type lamps	3200 K	Type B or tungsten-type (3200 K) color films.
1000-watt tungsten lamp	3000 K	
Enlarger lamps, 211, 212, 302[3]	2980 K	Anscochrome Printon, Kodak Color Print Materials Type C and Type R, Ektacolor Print Film, and Ansco Color Duplicating Films Type 538 and Type 638.
Household lamp, 500-watt	2950 K	
Household lamp, 100-watt	2865 K	
Household lamp, 60-watt	2800 K	

[1] Considerable variation in color temperature; check with manufacturer of unit. Without filter, a rendition generally tends to be on the cold side.

[2] SM and SF lamps recommended for Type A film only.

[3] When used with heat-absorbing glass in enlarger or over light source.